Da Grustle

1 MILLION IN THE MAKING

Eric Alan Cominski Jr

I dedicate this book to…

To all hard-working entrepreneurs that are taking on the fear of being your own

My friends & Family

My Legacy

Battle King Inc.

Table of Contents

Chapter 1 1

Chapter 2 21

Chapter 3 35

Chapter 4 49

Chapter 5 59

Chapter 6 81

Chapter 7 95

Chapter 8 107

Chapter 9 117

Chapter 10 129

"TOMMOROW SUCCESS BEGANS TODAY"

Frank Schaffer

Chapter 1

AS I BEGIN to write this episode of my life, I realized how far I had come. The mountains I have had to climb, the oceans I sailed, the end I have had to believe is true even when it does not seem so. It is true what they say, "life is very short, and you can either live it or have someone live it for you". Then a beam of smile fell upon my face and great joy surfaced. Then I said to myself, "Till this point, I am convinced I have lived my life". I have made every choice my way - both the bad and good, I am to be blamed. I had gone through everything myself, so refreshing. But not everyone responds to this blossom of reflection with a smile. When asked, they respond with a shrug that they have endured. Truth be told, life is not meant to be endured but lived and loved. So, have you lived life for yourself and with love? In the years that separate birth from death, you would come to find your answers written across times. My story would not be as dramatic as that of Cinderella and Harry Potter. But it is also not without life. My mother didn't die when I was little, but she married a man that wasn't my birth father. I wouldn't have a family that hated me, as far as I know anyway. I also wouldn't have a beginning like that of Harry whose both parents died and was made to stay with his Aunt and Uncle who detests his parent and what they believed. I wouldn't have that. But I sort of have my own dramatic part. I have a story to tell about how we were separated; I have a story about how we were pulled apart and I had to live through it all. I have a story – which if I tell it in a particular manner, it could be dramatic.

When we look back and realize the change that has befallen us, we are bound to celebrate it or berate it. Our motivation - to either celebrate or berate - is not karma, but our response to karma. As for me I have lived – still living – and answered some of the life questions, and in my little years, I have seen the gloomy days that seemed to never go out, and the tormenting fire that felt like it has come to stay. But all through this, I was above. Then this I conclude, "Life is so dangerous it can be fruitful, that in life itself –forgetting all the pain – we would realize that the diamonds of excellence are dwelling beneath if only we would all persevere". Trenton, the city, where I was birthed in has grown in its own glory – or I would rather say gloomed into the darker further. From the stands at the edges of the city to the magnanimous center, everything has changed.

I asked myself, "Is this the same city?" The answer was clearly written before me, it is and at the same time it is not – what a paradox! C'est la vie! This is Trenton, the city of my beginnings, so much has changed since the last time I saw you. The city which came to be around in the 17th century has been marked by so much history that its dissertation would seem to know no end. Yeah, still maintains the capital of New Jersey, but its wind is not the fresh breath it once was. William Trent, from whom the name was derived, has built this city on wealth and success. And now, the gates seem to be over the edge, we have been identified with danger in more ways than ever. Though we could never stop the present from not happening, our glorified past should bear a mark on us. When it started Trenton was a source of hope to many, many immigrants from Europe came to jolly in its wealth. Italians, Hungarians, the Jewish and the Polish…all trail in to enjoy. Little did we know we would soon fall into dissent. It was in this city that one of the world greatest civil right activists, Martin Luther King Jr., would face his demise, a stain that would forever bear its markers on our garment. Trenton! "Trenton Makes, the World Takes". At one time we were a big player in the Industrial Revolution. Now we commute in so much pain to the extent that our garden grows old in the daytime. It is not that the city has gone to sleep, No, far from it. It just happened that the toil is not wholesome to be awesome. At night, we may look at the day's work and be on top of the world, but the world grew bigger than we thought. The atmosphere is without hesitation a taste of splendor. Winters are cold and damp; summers are hot and humid. The gentle breeze and slight head of humidity make your day. In our struggle, we simmer in the moment; too beautiful to not look at. Such a clean slate you would imagine? But it is not so we have grown to be dangerous, "Will" I envisioned will be concerned at the future we are driving at, the crime across the city makes the paper –an evidential fact is the presence of two maximum prisons in the county. Its history had overtime sunk and men forgot the honorable part, making it a very hard city to leave in. The truth does not also shy away from the fact that we had history and the joy of being related to the roots of American independence –speaking of the Battle of Trenton –is, without doubt, an awesome satisfaction that we mean something the American states. Coming home, I begin the journey of my family. "Blood is thicker than water", sure enough, that's always right –never been wrong for me though, or has it for you? And family; a lively phenomenon that makes us all become crazy or go the extremes, whichever we choose still does not defer our blood link.

My family has been there for me – right from the start –a peek into the past I would not still change anything about them. I would grow to become a fine young man –the words of my mother –through the shadows cast on me from my family. Family! Family! I sat down to reminisce on the smooth beginning I witnessed –I was not always there from the beginning if you know what I mean. Joy encompassed me as I remember the days that went without a laugh, the ones that came with a smack, the ones that were hilarious – I would recount these moments with my siblings and we would laugh it out. We, my family were not too big a family as other families in those days. Furthermore, I was the only son in the family –lots of prestige, right? The order, if I can remember was: two sisters before me –my mom would later give birth to a sister after me. Why it happened, I cannot say, "it just happened to be so", that was the answer I got when I asked the childish question of why I was the only son. As a little boy, I was bottled with myself, the other male figure in the house was my Dad –whom you will later meet –and he was not always around. The other option was to play with the girls, which I surely wouldn't do, any day and any time –no offenses there my sisters. So far for me, my early years were boring and kind of exciting for my sisters if you ask me. We grew in our little abode and the town also grew to be more dangerous –no one could pinpoint that moment, but things happen, right? The town was living in hell with continuous surge in crime rate; there was no clear consensus on how we could manage to stay afloat amid these. But we managed. I would remember those days that a walk in the park was lesser than never when we could have envied from the housetops and do not dare walk in. Now that I look back, I realized that everything was changing faster than we could catch up with; I can only thank my mom for being able to separate us from the remaining pack. We tried to live different from the rest of the pack, but one could only try. Trenton, I would agree was a tough place to live. But it formed me. Someone once said, "If they don't break you, they make you". Trenton didn't break me, –I left in one piece, or should I say I left before I could drift away –it made me. But the story was different from the man of the family, as much as we tried to not be part, he pulled us in. My father to me was a hard man to live with, maybe due to his history or due to his roots –he was from the suburbs that hurt. To be candid, it was not that he made the day hell for us, but I always knew he could do better. It was hurting me seeing the other man in the house being drawn away from me –the only person I would have loved to relate with. I soon accept that he was not with the family; he had drifted off.

As children, we hoped all day that we would have the nice little dream family, but each day reality dawns on us and our hopes were being cemented every hour rather than awakened. The jail was one of the ways my father kept bringing us back. I couldn't quite say maybe it was the jail that wouldn't let him go or that my father was fond of the jail, this I cannot tell. But one seems to be fond of the other, right? Because how would you explain the frequent visitation to the County Police Department and they [Police] appear to also be convenient with it. Yeah, it was not that our trips to the station were on severe accusations, but they were never befitting to learn from as my mom would put it –this I agree with. "You've got to stay out of trouble", my mother would say. She just couldn't reconcile with the fact that those [my dad and her] who enjoined us to stay out of trouble would be the reason for one to visit police station. There were times, I would assume when mom would be scolding us in the present of Dad just to get her message through even though the message was not meant for us but for dad. She is a wise woman. It was without question that my father is not the easiest person to go by, but his way to lead us out of the way was the pain in my mom's neck. Life without trouble was unbearable, now laying it with one was totally a wreck for the family. Though, he was a saddle of bad news, my Dad was and still is a good person –even to this day I still get in touch with him. Often, when Dad is free from one trouble, he takes into the good-husband-tux. He becomes the father of the year, you could hardly say what would have been next, but before we know it, he is back in. We could only wonder why he was like that. Can't he just be the good guy forever? Why won't he just stay out of trouble? But if you've lived in my hood, you would know to stay out of trouble was almost superficial –not that I embrace what he has done, just stating the facts. The town says trouble, we all agreed, but we all wanted one family, and the way my dad was going about getting arrested day in day out was not going to make us one big happy family. It was always a sore sight to see a mother assiduously working to keep the family together. Her long last love is now long lost, a sight not to be held by any mother. "He was not like this when we met", those were the words of my mom when the load felt too heavy. At this point, I realized how well I need to be there for my mom. Her tears had always been a pain in my heart; I would give anything to give her joy. I did my best to help her, but I felt helpless I couldn't do that one thing that made the whole thing go away – convince my dad to stop. All I could do was cry with her, sympathize with her…that was the only language I understood. But time was going, and something needed to be done quickly.

It is nearing the cliff, the driver was heading straight for destruction, he is ready to fall off the edge, but if the driver would not hear the cry of the others, jumping off is not unfair. So was the situation of our family, mom could not stand it anymore, we all couldn't bear it anymore, it was becoming gruesome, so we had to leave. I could not have agreed more that leaving a problem might not be the solution to that problem, but in this case, there was no other option. "I am laying down now, so I could fight a better day", those were the words from over the radio assuring us that we are meant to leave some fights. Not that they are not worth fighting over, but that we will surely have something more to lose if we fight. How did that happen? All through the period that dad was moving in and out of the jail, they never stopped loving each other –I still believe to this day they didn't. Till this day, I am baffled at this extent of love they both showed. This is the love that soothes the pain and still scolds the action. How much I wanted this love –to be loved and love someone in such manner. Mom's resolution to move was never vindictive; rather it was a need-to-do scenario. It was a tough choice, but she took it. She blew the final whistle. I was still very small at this time – about four years of age –I can only envision how the interaction would have gone when mom told Dad we were leaving. I believe he would be defeated –mom was going to leave with everyone; he could plead but to no end, he was the cause. Dad would not welcome this departure with an open hand, but mom was not ready to let it lie, "this time around we are going", she told my dad. As the days that we were to leave become closer, dad became more available. He was doing his best, so we would not leave, but we needed his best earlier. Mom was not going to deny him time with his children but moving them out of Trenton was inevitable. When Dad came to the realization that nothing was going to change, he accepted and kissed us bye. The day, though blurring because I was little, I can remember the tears that flowed on our cheek. I couldn't quite understand it fully then, but I knew we were leaving dad. It was a goodbye we all needed. My mom would recount the episode of her departure to me in my later years. It was then that our little one big family split –not a bad split, but a one of understanding. My oldest sister lives in Georgia with her Dad, and my second oldest sister lives in Virginia with my grandma. We had a family which was willing to help us with the change. Virginia, as a little boy, I knew little about Virginia. I would later grow to know its history and fall in love with this town and in this town. Virginia in its own glory I beheld you the day I moved in. Day after day, you amaze me. Here in the depth of my domains, I salute thee, the "Mother of Presidents".

More than eight presidents have been birthed in this city, a state more than any other. Your elegance is breath-taking. This became the town I would know and love. Though I was a stranger, here I would grow and live my dreams. Now a grown man I can call this city my home. I have sojourned in this city, and the blessings have dwelt masterly on me. The city's beauty is revealed in its everyday sight. The humid temperature of the state was not a definite digression from New Jersey, as very cold in the early months of the year and temperatures rising by the month till the peak in the middle of the year, but something was different. The breath of the city was a new life for me and my mom –mom would tell that to me in later years. And I was sure I could feel it. It was clear where we came from is a clear contrast of where we are. I believe it should be a wise man, right? That said, "Where you are going should be better than where you are coming from", I think mom followed that. Life is going to get better. Though I moved, I didn't know what would happen in later years. I missed the familiar – Trenton. I still remember the days I wished we hadn't moved, and I still can tell of days that gave me great joy we moved. Mixed feelings, right? But it was needed. At some point in life, there is the need to leave the familiar and journey into the unknown. Those who have gone straight ahead belittling any fear have been known to come home with so much gain, and those who allowed the fear to cripple their ability to move on remained in their comfort zone without the ability to reach for the horizon. Then I realized the ability to move into the unknown is not a sign of recklessness but that of hope and strength that you would find the use for in later life. In a strange land, I have found myself. I would live it and so far, I have. Mom still went around with her daily business of mothering me. My younger sister and my oldest sister that stayed with grandma and I were the ones that were left with mom, so she had more time to spank our ass and scold our minds. When we moved mom told us, "life is not going to be different, nothing is going to change". At first, I thought, right, everything will be going the same way, but when reality hit me I soon discovered that everything was going to change. Even my mom. And this was the part something changed for her. She found love. Now I do not know what love is at this time, but I could tell when mom is happy, and she was –that's love for me then. She told me she had found someone – I cannot really tell then, I was rather new to all that. This happened before I got into middle school.

It was a table discussion I had with mom with her telling me how she had to move on in her life, I can't quite figure out why she told me all these, because she knew quite frankly that I did not understand any of the things she said, but she went on all the way. Though I never understood much of what she said then, sure I do now. She went on and on about a particular man, who she thinks might be her best fit…As a kid, all I could tell with all certainty was sadness, and joy on my mom's face, and as she described her relationship with the man, her face lit, she was different, and I wanted her to be like that. So, I just nodded, not that mom needed my permission to love, it was her way of telling me how much she loves me. Their relationship went on, the man proved to be a nice man, although I could not say why overall, he was good enough to join the family. That was then. If it were to be now, I am sure the man –soon to be your mother's boyfriend –would be drilled with loads of questions. But I was new to all these and it didn't seem much like a big deal to me. Whenever he comes around we have a good time together. I thought it would be good to be part of the family –I kept my thoughts to myself though. But maybe mom heard that thought, as she declared that the man would be joining the family –she was going to marry him.; Yeah marry him. It was so good to be little as all these never mattered much to me. Everything was as easy as saying yes or no if it made you happy or sad. Now when I am fully grown, and I have experienced a series of emotions, I must sieve through it all and everything is more complex. I was going to have a stepdad, and quite alright I have seen from movies, stepdad stories – the dad that is not your dad, was how I described it then. I have heard, as they would say it, the good, the bad and the ugly. It cringes me to think he would turn out to be a bad one. I prayed that he wouldn't and sure enough my prayers were answered. Mom also wanted him, and she as always looked out for me, why stop now? They got married and lived happily ever after – yeah it does still happen. As life began to unfold in my new world, I also had to step into it. I had to begin school. School a term derived from the Greek word schole originally meaning "leisure" – which is a rather contradicting to school, right? When I began to grow, and school system unfolded to me I began to grow indifferent towards the rewards it has promised from the beginning of age – learning. I would say my experiences redefined my knowledge of school into an infrastructure developed to mould one into one of its architecture. I soon realized how much school stripped me of many things which was nothing compared to what it later gave me. So, do I say schooling is bad?

Far from it. The truth be told, school was never intended to hurt, but the hurt that stems from it is a product of its configuration -the system. At Virginia, after I graduated elementary I got admitted into one of the middle schools in the neighborhood, I needed to get out of the box and experience life. Good education and a good school, an unclear relation we would be unfair to dabble in it. In my early years, good school, to the best of my knowledge, should provide a good education – which is so in a lot of cases. But there are always exceptions. My advice is to watch out. A good education is needed to be a very fine, respectable man, and everyone went on how good school would be. Education, I was not against, but If the school was synonymous with success, I have seen, then everyone who went to school will command success. In my little years, I have seen how neighbors fare in their daily life, even though they have the very much pressured schooling. I began school as required of me, but the end of school days was always on my mind. I looked forward to the day I would leave the four walls of the school on the very day I entered. It lacked the adventure I so much hoped for. I did my best to fulfill all the routines needed to be in school, but I had a nonchalant attitude towards school. I did not take school seriously not for the fact that school was irrelevant, but that school was a bunch of regulations and procedure to be fulfilled. School, I tell you would be fun if it were more adaptive and flexible, but it wasn't. Though I was not satisfied, I cannot have my way. Brainy? No, but I was great at Math, Science and Physical Education. So, was I indifferent towards school because of my intelligence? NO. I was indifferent from the start, one would say my tickling of life did not fall in this direction. I would soon realize that diagnose was true. But there was something I was good at, keeping clean. Being the face that moves others was my goal – if you cannot get the grades, why not get the girls. Then, I had no apparent understanding of getting attention, but the feeling was good. I chose to be classy; I invested enough time in my act so the boy from Trenton may be popular. From my hair to my cloth to how I handle things down to how I walked, I aimed to be like a solo in an Italian concert – everyone must notice. All of me was to be popular, the school was a bye. I would wake up early not to get my homework check – well I did when the complaints were getting too much – but to check my clothing for the day. I took my time to polish my appearance to the fullest. All the while, I did this to be popular not knowing what it would amount to. A grown man now, I realized how those moments formed me. The time I took to take care of myself is telling now. How better it would be if men could know what will happen if they did certain actions? The truth, we can never know.

We can just maximize the time and pray we did it right. And so was my life in middle school. A young me, with a lot of things to hope for and dreams I could surmount, settled for improving myself rather than face school squarely like a brick wall. At a tender age, I had begun to live for myself. Though I would not applaud this attitude of mine, I would not berate it either, because as long as I live I would tell of these moments in joy. It was no surprise to me when I finished middle school with all D's. In those days, grades were a tell of how good a school was rather than the student. But this was not the school, everyone knew, this was me. The reports were sent to our parents as they knew some of us –including me – would just give a mouth report, and mouth reports are never good. When the reports were sent to my mom, it was a bad sight. I pass with all Ds. The day the school sent the result over; I came home as the joy of finishing middle school was in me. As I opened the door and saw the firm look on my mom's face, I knew something was wrong.

Step Dad, I should mention was a navy, and mom was a nurse. She had a night shift, the previous night and was on her "recovering rest" when the result came in. I tried to figure out what could be wrong: Did I not take out the garbage? Did I not put the appropriate clothes in the laundry...it took me a while to realize that it could be the result? And all the while I was in my thinking mood her firm look didn't seem to shift, she meant business. She brought up the sheet which had been laying on the table – the other chairs had been obscuring it from my view – and showed me. "They sent your result", she said, "and look what I found", she continued. It was all D's. Mom was surprised, but I wasn't, and I was not going to show it. At that instant, I change my countenance, and then she became concerned, after all, I am my mother's son. When becomes very disturbed by a scenario, or she dislikes what she has seen, she expects a sad countenance, it was her way of knowing I was sorry. So, I left all the "popularity drill" and fell into the countenance of mom's boy who is sorry and would be better next time. I did not need to say anything as mom did not utter anymore after, maybe she was tired, I could not say. I was relaxed, I did expect some level of wrath to come down, but nothing seems to be happening, to me this was below expectation. Don't get me wrong, Mom is a strong woman, but not tough. I would believe she was thinking after which she looked up and gave me such a displeasing nod which indicated that I was at least going to get to go to high school. I would bear it in my mind, but I was still expecting more wrath to come down. I was sure I have faulted. Then she bent her head again, like there was something more and then there was silence. I just stood there expecting whatever may come next.

After several minutes of silence and concerning look – I can't say for sure what thought run through her mind then, but now as a father, I have pretty much an idea of what may be happening. She stood and walked into her room. Her look of displeasure burned through my guts through the night even though the feeling of going to high school was jolting a new energy in me. I was indeed sorry. I would do my best to be better than this in high school, signed sincerely your only son. After a long summer, I got into high school. My lifelong need for maturity is soon to be within reach. I have seen how high school students rolled in the neighborhood, and I am deemed to take part in it. I believed high school would blow my mind. High school, I assumed, is purposed to be different from middle school I presumed. I would never know what to believe until I resumed the first day. Yes, high school was different: the edifice, the population, the arrangement, but at the end of it, I realized we were still in the same loop. The same rigid regulations, school work, rules, teachers – an old blood. I was a bit disappointed; the zeal of entering high school was regressed. All through middle school, I have envisioned a high school that would be less of set-by motions. In years later, I found out that it was not that high school was not different some pointed out it matched their expectation, it was that I had no expectations of how high school would be like. I did not have any hopes of what I wanted more, so life in high school was more of a continuous loop I feared than a glorious departure I wanted. So, it got me thinking, can a person be hoping for a future without an expectation? Yes. And is it healthy? No. I believe our expectations are what guide us to see the future we so much want. If we have no expectation of what we want in the future, when the future comes we may never know. It is thus high time, we stopped believing in the future without an expectation and start hoping for a future expectantly. I had no hopes, so I couldn't know if my hopes were met. Thus, I feared I might have been duped into believing the high school was really high. With this kind of mind, I attended classes; a mature man who is a bit disappointed. With time, my disappointment grew into complacency -the next on the list was tyranny, but I was not going near it – that every "schoolmaster" wanted me ousted of his class before his arrival. My complacency was not without disturbance of my mom at work. She got calls not very often to be depressed but it was enough for her to give me bedtime good-behavior-suits story. I just couldn't help it, I tried my best not to care more about school work, but it just was not working. Amid all this sagginess of mine, I was still a good boy, the lessons from my father still bore itself in me.

My stepdad as before was trying his best to be around at the time of my "prime energy", as my teachers described it to my mom, but never blame the man for his job. It was not that I was a rebellion, nor was I planning to be one, I was just not satisfied. Some of my teachers do call me to give me their 'honest advice' they would say, but I wanted more than they could offer every day. The definite answer to my quest, that I wanted more, was oblivious rather than obvious. Advice, information, encouragement came from all sides, I would not deter. And with time they all came to a halt, I was gone. I grew from the boy teachers were concerned about to the boy they do not care about. I was not also helping it. I was as before as unconcerned as one can be. Not only had the teachers, people around me [neighbors] begun to say things. As a young boy, I tried to be a bit better, but not too good to be untrue. I did my fair part in the community growth but did not care who cared about my actions. I was not one of those that would damage the courtyard grass, but I was the one who would see the fun in it. People started to berate me on self-expression, to them I was a young man, who had a whole life ahead of him, they commented, "I should not live like this and that …". I was sure if they had their way, they would all have agreed to tutor me day in day out on the outcome of my actions – which were unknown to me at that point. I for one also knew my actions were some at most times unjustifiable, I was sure to some greater extent that, many of my actions were uncalled for, I could only care less. The need to get out of the expectant loop was looming on me daily. Every day, I succumb to the stress of the high school education, then they would also want me to yield to the "congress-neighborhood-discipline", I decided to say no. In later years, I would look back at these days and recount it to my children to get a better of myself I couldn't get then. In my high school years, even though I berate the system, I learned of a life-changing phenomenon, "entrepreneur". It was in one the classes I so much detested, but on this fateful day, I happened to be concerned. The term seems to be the answer I was looking for. On this day, I did my best to stay in class throughout. After the class, thoughts ran through my head of how to begin on this part. It was sure I couldn't go to the teachers to ask for more insights, as it would turn to be another section of lots of insults in advice and advice in insults – that sort of thing is common. It was around this time that my mom called me and told me to get a job. That right there was the reality showing his face. I knew when I see him – then I didn't, now I know. I was always certain that at one point, I had to get a job; I have seen others do it, why should mine be different.

"I would have to cut back helping you with spending", she said, "and in the long run you will thank me for it", she added. Thank you? Right then all I could think of were why now. I tried to understand, so I asked, "Why mom?" she told me it was high time I began to live with responsibilities, how I needed to learn to do for myself. This was going to be new because if I could remember my mom and dad were always there, hearing they would drawback was a bit to take in for me – a spoilt young boy. Within me, I was filled with mixed feelings: sad that I would not have a mom to go back to, and excited that I could go on to make some money for myself. Was I to thank her or not, I could not decide – who thanks his parent for cutting on his spending? In search of the job, I had to do more, largely because my reputation precedes me. I scurried across the coast of the city searching helplessly for one that could suit the man I had become. With days of combing, I finally found a fast food restaurant, Popeye's; theirs was a fried chicken fast food, whose manager was willing to add this young blood to those already in. In those days, it was not uncommon to find young men and women work in fast food, attend at supermarket. The neighborhood was safe, which I think was among the reasons, young guys and girls could do this; at another place, the story would have been different. When men and women in their late fifties onward see a young man or lady at any one of these places, they all tend to dispense their own source of wisdom to them, that they made one of the best decisions and lots of unsolicited advice. And most time, the person is said to have no option but to stay and nod as respect was what they wanted and not giving them would result in the manager knowing, you don't want to know what comes after. I met the manager, a man in his mid-forties, not built to be called a gymnast, dressed in a pale close to a cream shirt and gray-colored trousers, with suspenders and a broad-sized white polka dot tie. He was a man from the classic. His smell was indistinguishable from that of the restaurant, thus I concluded he was not a fan of the fragrance. His face told of his past than his future, he was a stern man, probably being involved in one of those wars' men fought – which war? How could I know; never asked him - and had come back home, I could not figure out that part out exactly. He gave me a straight long look which to avoid I looked about the room as a man searching for something, and thus I noticed how small the office was and how arranged he was, he was a man who knew what he wanted. After few minutes of silence, he spoke, his deep calm voice, like that of bassist, I recognized authority in his voice, this was a man who had gone far, I need to be on my best behavior, I told myself.

He told me how he respected that men of my age could still come to look for the job, he reminded me that most of the people I would be working with are of my age, and at the close, he gave me a long standing of things he would accept and those he would not. In the end, I have a job. In my search for the job, I had journeyed to the end of the road which resulted in me taking a bike to work every day. I did not like the fact that it was long, but the distance was something I desired. I needed to leave the familiar. This experience I was certain will mark a turning point in my life. Every time I rode to work, the gentle breeze gives me a feel of how beautiful life is, I had been staring at life through the lenses of my school teachers, but a new world I began to explore every day at my job. The job was satisfactory for a man of my age, what more could I have wanted? Mom was relieved, "Her son has a job!". I was also happy with the job, new people, new environment, but I wanted more. I wasn't certain then, the source of my thirst for more. Now, I could only say, it was because of the things I have seen which had unconsciously forged my decision-making capabilities. I have seen a hardworking man in dire need when he thought he had everything. It was not that the money being paid was not enough; I was not leaving on my own yet, I had no bills to pay, I just felt within me the need to have more money. I realized this was partly due to the fact of my encounter with the word "entrepreneur" and my confirmation that I was not one, or that I wanted so much to elude living above average. I do not want my life to be based on a few bucks from one who thinks he is doing me the favor by paying. I fared well in my new job which was quite amazing. But all the while I still felt the thirst, more needed to come. I have seen and heard people say that "a thirst for more might be endless". I wouldn't disagree with this and some even went further to tell us that the endless nature of this thirst may be destructive. That also, a good point. But I also think we should always ask for more, if we have it, we are in gain, if we don't we don't die over it. I was pressed on having more and nothing was going to stop my pressing further. I would go to school and then head for my job after school hours. School hours I berated, office hours I anticipated. In school, I was thinking of making money. Which is not what I would advise. Face your studies, and get a good education, that's my advice. Nothing is a good substitute for good education. Yeah, not everybody needs to fully focus to get what is needed, some are gifted. My advice, know thyself, and when you do work thyself and you eventually get to the top, always remember who you were before you get to that position. Never be lost in the moment.

Thoughts and ways ran through my mind, it was like piles of paper flung from a height with each going its way according to the wind. Idea after idea hit me. It is true what they say, "Millions are the idea, and the multi-million ones are the most rare ones". Each idea on top of the other that was when I started to pen my idea down, "the faintest ink is better than the sharpest memory". I got an idea book to document the memories of ways that come across my mind. In the process, I got an idea that if one person had done something and it works, why not try that same thing and see if it would work. So, I began to look out for how people made money, and with the wealth of people I saw daily – at Popeye – I decided to learn. Each day, at home, school or at work, I learned of people who were making their money themselves not from the government – not that I could not learn from those working for the government. And this I found out; those who work privately are best equipped with the information I needed. I took every opportunity I had, every corporate dressed fellow who converse in the language of respect, whose appearance sprout satisfaction, not that I could always tell, was a friend of mind. I took care of their order to the nearest extreme, become friends with them in the limited time that I had, and got to know how they reached their present stage. Many of the individuals I met were very happy to help, they went to great lengths of offering their candid advice, and some even dropped off their numbers so I could reach out to them. Over time I had made friends with almost every "suit-wearing fellow" that came through the door of Popeye. A fateful incident led to my voyage. I would remember it for years to come. In high schools' days, you could either bring your lunch or get served in the school cafeteria, and the queue was usually long that many who could live without the lunch would do so. Then there was this guy, looks pale but seems to be the well-fed type – as you know in the typical school setting, there is the reasonably fed guy, who looks slim, the overfed guy, is fat and mostly with a ponytail, and there is the underfed guy, looks thinner than usual and is always the first to finish his lunch. He approached and told me how he forgot his lunch and went on about how he could not join the queue as it was too long for him or did not want the school food, it was not clear, he was one of the guys whose accent sounds like one speaking with few of his teeth missing. I had bought a pack of candy to school on this day, one of many days I decide to go off the diet as my mom was always a stickler for dietary. He offered to buy my pack of candy which I refused, thus he went on and on and raised his offer to buy my candy for $6. This was the candy I bought for $3, now I would be making a 100% profit. I made certain he was desperate as I did not want any trouble.

He was stiff on paying me six dollars for my candy. I was happy, a nice deal I said to myself, but all the while I never showed this rather I put on the face that I am just doing this for you as a friend to another. On getting the candy from me he leaped with a sign of accomplishment, he was convinced he had bargained and got a good deal. Then the unordered thoughts reordered, the thought on top of the pile hit me - should start selling candy. That was the beginning of my path to what would lead my search for more. I had made my first trade as a businessman, and my profit was 100% - though abnormal, I was happy with myself. The memories of this trade still burn in me as I teach others of the basic steps I took in making more money for myself and building an exotic business.

"WHEN THINGS CHANGE DON'T COMPLAIN JUST MAKE ADJUSTMENTS AND KEEP MOVING"

Eric Cominski Jr

Chapter 2

RIGHT THEN, unofficially official, I started selling candy. This moment led me to one of the best encounters I would have to start a business. I have heard it's hard starting a business, and for a high school student, it's a lot harder believe me. When I started, it didn't quite occur to me that I was starting a business – at least not in a formal way. I just got the idea of selling candy, at a reasonable amount and the knowledge from Popeye's executive told me it was a good thing. I was happy with myself. Back at home, I couldn't tell them what was fully going on at school, not that mom would dissuade me, but I am sure she would not agree completely. I was still in high school for God's sake. So, I did my best to be discrete. I could only try as my activities of buying candy from the main street to sell in school became obvious – my school pack became bigger. Every now and then, I would get the "something is wrong, you are not telling me something." look from mom, and I would give her the "nothing is wrong, everything is absolute!" She would later find out in later years; I might have blurted out over one of our dinners. Every day at school promised a big sale, the other students were big on buying. It was not until I started selling candy, I never knew there were many of the students who also did not feel the school food was good enough for them, or that the queue at the cafeteria could be "killing", as one of the guys would describe it. I got a reasonably share of profit from this adventure not as much profit as I got from my first sale. It was a decent cut. All the while the activities of my selling needed to be unheard of, so I did my best to ensure enough discretion to be undetected. I do not want another excuse for a fellowship of advice. Every time someone would walk up to me to buy candy. I smiled at myself, not for the money part but because I was solving a problem. I did my best to enjoy every moment. This was when it started to appear clear to me that if there is a problem to be solved and there is someone around to solve it, success is inevitably at the corner. At that time, I could not see the bigger picture, I was still new to this, but I did not stop growing. I look back at my innocent self then and I realize how much bad choices I started making during that time, even though it seems like a good one. The fun thing is that I enjoyed every part of it. My piggy bank was growing, I was becoming extra cool, I was getting along with everyone. I became popular then – a thing we all need at some point. Even with all the segregation and clique in high school.

I could meddle with everyone, it was so cool because right from time, I had been a loner – not a life I chose, but what life brought out of me, I didn't have a lot of friends. I would later realize that my lack of friends was because of the fear I have of losing them. I had experience separation at one time with my dad, and I was not planning on going on another toll anytime soon. So, I did my best to stay cool, the type of cool that doesn't freak everyone out and still doesn't create a gang for itself – I was business cool. I did a lot of trading and I was getting good by the day. I also lost a lot of money and made a lot of gains. I had known right from the start that it was not going to be easy. I was not also going to take the easy way out. School on the other end was suffering. I tried – I think I did, but it was not easy and my disdain for the strict system was not helping. I still got by with math and physical education, but the rest were kicking my butt. Sometimes I got thinking, what if I had no business? Was I going to fare well? I discovered I might not, some of us aren't just built for such type of thing – I wasn't. Now I had two streams of money, my job and selling candy. Can a man ever be satisfied? Are you satisfied? Still, at this stage in my life, I still don't feel satisfied. Is it a disease? It would have been if only a few of us have it, but my interaction with life has shown that we all have it, that unfulfilled desire of us. Desire is what keeps us living, help us make choices day after day. Our desire to own a car pushes us to work, our desire to vote the right person in compels us to watch them manifest. And if we stop desiring we would continue to run aimlessly and that's when we start dying. Basic empowerment 101 tells us how fundamental our desire can affect our view of this everyday life. Yeah, some of your desires might go unfulfilled. But that day we don't desire, we would never produce. I also realized that from the age of men to the dawn of time, man had strived to achieve better than yesterday. I have seen and can say with enough certainty that man was not built to be satisfied. This is evident in how far we have come from the Stone Age to Iron Age down to the industrial revolution and now in the internet age. Man has struggled to meet his desire. John F. Kennedy's desire to put a man on the moon drove the United States to the peak in the space race. We have always strived to achieve better results. Everywhere I went I see man demanding to get more. In the offices, through the streets, everywhere there is the clamor for more. As I continued to brood on satisfaction with man. I stumbled on an answer which was so real to me, he said, "it was a life that demanded more from them and that was why we want more". Life? Demanding more? How could it be?

My yearning could still not be contained so I continued. I directed my questions towards life, why does life want more? Why was the provision of yesterday not enough? I looked, and this is what I found, "the changing of time". I found out that time went on changing, and each change demands some corresponding quantities of dedication. Life works on direct proportionality basics, an increase in a variable necessitates an appropriate increase in the other, and so is life. We live through life as it changes, the seasons become colder, and we get thicker sweaters. The tax becomes higher, we get higher sales. The job becomes well; we secure it. Thus, this is my conclusion, life demands and we all must subject to its demand. And it [life] demands more because there is and will always be some type of change and that man, in order, to live life you must provide more to fulfill the demand of life. Change leads to more demands from life, which eventually leads to the need to want more. Candy business was going well but I could still do more, and I wanted more. I had blood flowing through my veins which could execute almost any idea I throw at it. I was still in my early years, and I was learning a lot as business and life were teaching me a load. My thirst for more – not an unhealthy one – was driving me to think of so many things a guy of my age shouldn't be thinking yet. But who sets the line for this sought of thinking? The society has been poised to believe I can't think more than a certain way. I was not going to let the society hinder me. I was going to out-think the society, and that I eventually accomplished. About my time in high school, we were moving towards the internet age: landlines where departing for mobile phones, each home was growing with PCs and life was getting easier. VCRs and Radios were becoming less of a household must have as the new DVD players were in town. And as one would have envisioned, the entire technology sphere was still new, so many people faulted into thinking they knew a lot. A giant misappropriation in human life. The greatest obstacle I have seen in people is the fact that they know so much that they know nothing. I have met with a different set of people, I realized that our ability to be great at what we do is embodied in our strength to learn, unlearn and relearn. If you can't, no one is going to offer you a place in this new world. CDs and DVDs were growing in my area, many had a DVD & CD Players and there was a need for music and movies. Not many people were really good at burning music & movies, I figured there were so many because of the surge and so few expertise because many didn't even know anything about it.

To me, they were trying to solve a problem not at the expense of a solution, but at the expense of the prize [money]. The need was there, many people needed to burn CDs and they did well to take it to the so-called expert only to be disappointed in return. Many of those that patronize these people continue to blab about how they got a new CD and within days of using it, it stops working or that it was just behaving "kind of funny", I recalled one of our customers telling a colleague of his over the table. CDs and DVDs were going to be my next stop. I not only want to solve this problem for the sake of the prize, but I was angered at how unnatural those who proffer solutions seemed to care less than expected. It was a definitive move for me. I wanted to step up and do him good. Then I began to research on this [CDs and DVDs]. When I was learning about how people made their money, the knowledge that was instilled in me was, "the knowledge of a business is very paramount to the success of the business". This I have used from the moment I started out till today. "You need to know what makes you the money to make the money", one of my advisers said. I went on to research on the topics; about creating CDs, its history, how it was different. I did my due diligence to help me excel in making a better product. I was in my mid-teens now, but I understood the very concepts that made business rise and fall. Knowledge that differentiates. After everything, I had to come back, I was still in high school, but I was long lost from school work. I remembered times, I found out about a class project or assignment on the day of submission, but I believed my high school days in the academic sphere were better than that in my middle school days. I was mature then, and it did show forth in how I handle most of my subjects. I know quite alright that, my excellence in high school was not because I became serious, but that I was grown. Now is knowledge associated with growth? I believe yes. I can't put a scientific explanation on it, but something in me believes I am right. When you grow, you get a sense of knowing more things even though you never learnt them, you unconsciously become more equipped as your senses become more enlightened. It is just that we don't realize this innate ability of ours before it's too late. I had become a full-time hustler, candies and CDs and DVDs at school, Popeye after school. My entire focus was on my side hustles. I cannot say I was a good manager of time, because my academic suffered, but I did manage my candy and CDs sales with a very good front and was low-key to help avoid the very unfamiliar question, "what is this you are doing with your life?" this was a question man of my age was asked very often. I bet it is still being asked a lot these days. I should note that I did not officially start a business. No, there were loads of legalities to get through. It was enough to get a name, get it registered, the LLC Limited Liability Corporation, the permits, and all sorts, so I had an unofficial business, or let's just say I was selling. Money that I wanted was streaming in, and I was not an unconditioned guy that used everything he makes to enjoy the flow of life. I always want to be rich, but I believe in wealth through hard work, I believe I should have enough money and that the money needs to keep increasing up to a certain point, that point I did not know, and I was sure the point was not then, so I kept making money. My life has a high school student is not without the need to be free. I was not heavy on parties or drinking or any of the things a typical American Dad and Mom would need to worry about. I cannot say for certain why I was like that. Most of my colleagues were involved in some sort of high school sensations or the other. I was just not built for this kind of thing I would tell friends, "It's not my thing bro". This is not to say I did not go to parties – why wouldn't I? – I only went and stayed if the party is a way to meet interesting people. When I started realizing how far meeting people could go, I was always on the lookout to meet new faces daily. It was a source of great joy for me when I found someone interesting. Connection, that what it is called. You need to be connected to stay connected. You've probably heard of the adage that says, "no one is an island of knowledge". You should stick very well to it. I would later see the effect in my later years, I can't say everyone you meet will be worth it, but I am sure you would learn. I would get to parties, say hi to the host and look for a company. By the time, the new company I made started to leave, I also find myself a way home. Meeting new people was always my goal when invited to a party. I always do my best to scan through the crowd and look for people, detached from the rest of the party, and associate with them. As a young guy, I love to relate to other guys who demonstrate a considerable level of wisdom and who look like someone that have his shit together. MODELING…yeah, Modeling. The one thing my mom got me into was Modeling. It became a thing for me in high school also. Little did I know that all my acts in middle school would force me into becoming a wonderful- showman. Modeling to me was a way to act out my figure. Early on in my life, I was a big duty man, I had a routine for keeping myself fit. I went to the gym occasionally to get in shape and I kept myself clean to look well, as someone said, "you look good to feel good, and you look good to talk good". I understood the fact that your appearance is your first impression. So, all through my middle school and throughout my time in high school, I always engaged myself in activities that would get me in shape; mostly sporting activities.

I got a job as a model in Maryland DC which located northeast of Virginia and about 4-hour drive from Virginia to Maryland. I took trips back and forth between Maryland and Virginia during the weekends to do my job as a model. My mom was a rock on which I stood at that point, she helped me out when she could, driving upstate was stressful enough, and now for a nurse who is always stressed from a job it was more than stressful. Modeling taught me a lot about image. Images are great, but they can be superficial. I might look entirely different when they result is shown, it was a construction of me. I was going to be known not for who I am, but how I looked. As at the time, it didn't mean much to me, but now it certainly did. I had to be true to myself as I moved on in life, it was either I represent the image totally or the image represents me totally – no contradictions. Also, when I started modeling, people perceptions of me begin to change – I brought most of my works home. My image was speaking a language of respect and I lived in that moment, it might not be for long. Modeling was not a career path for me. Modeling in Maryland was quite stressful coming from Virginia. Maryland DC, "Maryland of Opportunity", a small state and the birthplace of the US anthem. With a weather, not distinctly different from Virginia, the limited amount of time I spent in this city is always to be remembered. The scenery was a sight to be seen and loved. I traveled to Maryland mostly by car – which mom drove. At Maryland, I was given a script to follow which I did to the best of my abilities. I was a budding model and I was privileged to get work with lots of agencies. I was sure I had walked in front of many model agencies to be able to tell which one was which. I had been scripted to walk in front of top agencies like Nickelodeon, top model, Disney, H & M, VH1 etc. One of the things about being a model is the attention you get from everyone on set, at times it can be intriguing and at other times it can be disturbing. Every job has its own pros and cons, right? It is necessary to point out that my mom was extremely happy with my choice to model. She had a thing for modeling, and her boy doing it was like she was the one doing it. I also did like modeling, but her push meant more to me. Even though, she was a bit occupied she made time to be available to take me to Maryland. Typically, a model, my day went like this; I get to go to the modeling agencies, meet with the Creative Director, the executive creative director or both, who would, with the help of the team, explain to me how I was to act, move or position myself. I was read a long script of how to do everything in a strategic manner, at some agencies, the details were overwhelming, I could barely remember the essential steps.

After that, I would begin and continue until I got it, at times I was given enough time to get the part right and at other times I needed to get it right then. With lots of people in modeling, one would think it was that easy, but it wasn't. There are times that the photoshoot would last up to more than a hundred clicks. In the end, I would become more tired than those who went for football practice. The director final speech – kind of a thing they do – is what signifies the end of the day. I mostly get a refreshing commentary from the director, I believe it was because I was still an up and coming model who might have a future and they do not want to ruin it with their cynicism. The lessons I learned from modeling would go on to tell on my interaction with people. I like modeling, but I was not going on it for a long time. I had more things in mind. All through high school, I had one love, which was music. When I started to model more, I got signed with AMG in a 4-year deal then after a while I started working on music. How did it begin? It all started with mix tape my dad sent from when he was locked up – I was still in touch with my father, I received letters and gifts from Dad when he was locked up. The song I listened to that picked my interest was the Rap song, "Money, Power, Respect" by the group called "The Lox". After I heard this song, I knew that was my eureka moment, right there I knew I wanted to make music. Music is a great work of art crafted out only by brilliant minds. We have seen, the history has told of the greats that billowed the flame of music to the standard it is today. And in every aspect of life, music has found its expression. It meaning I feared is a different story, as I have seen beautiful songs go understood and violated beyond its manifestations. I did my best to create and follow a music schedule for myself, besides my own busy schedule. I tried to be better with each song; I trained myself, at lunch breaks, both at school and at work. I spent many hours at home listening to any album I could lay hands on. Music to me, was a way of escaping, a way to be free. Whenever I listen to music, it is like my worries had flown away, all the wants and needs for more dried up, the lyrics in its own make marks on my mind, and like writing on the rock, it always stands for long. Ever heard that

"Music is a sooth for the soul". I believe this, and believe it is more than that, and more of a haven for the soul. A place where the soul could whisper to rest for him to come. I love music; the sound of multiples sources aggregating to do wonders. I like all genres of music, but I preferred some to some others. A favorite music enthusiast of mine once told me, "the music you listen to tells something about you". And I tried out to find which one of the genres was telling about me, and I found it to be more of Rap, hip-hop and less of blues and soul-searching songs.

I recognized with the rap life, it was, to me, a life of hustle, it was rough but beautiful – it is different. I listened to a lot of Rap music and memorized enough to sing along without as little as a breath. No one knew I loved to sing. I was sure my personality does not speak forth, a music lover. Music was my secret, it was what I deployed when things seem to be going out of hand with the candy, CDs, at Popeye or with modeling. I respected it and it came naturally to listen to it. The lyrics rang true in my ear than every advice I have ever heard. You can't truly help someone if you do not know what makes them tick. Then I knew most people couldn't help me out because, they did not understand my language, and the only one that did was a heart away. I trained myself well enough to be good, and I was, though I only listened to myself, I was confident I was good. Music gave me so much confidence. My need for confidence with each day can never be underestimated, so the need for confidence for everyone. We all need to be confident, about our choices, about our plans, that they would work out as planned. I was getting better with music. Music was also getting the better out of me. On one of my trips to Maryland, I went on to show my love for music. It was during one of the breaks I had. I decided to take a toll on one of the beats I heard on the way to the agency's booth. The beat kept ringing in my ear; I had to do something, so I began to put in a few words before I knew it I was brooding with attention. Not that I planned it or that I did not want it, I was in my zone. As the beat continued so did I and those around me joined in and welcomed the innocent voice they heard, many would later tell me how stylish it was. After a few rounds, I knew I had to finish, I would not want anyone to use my music as an act to chide me. With time, whenever I was on the break at some of the model agencies, I would hear a beat from those organizing the set, beats made using a table, or some sort of hard substance they could find. They wanted to listen to me more, they told me it was different and encouraged me to rap more for them. This was a welcomed change. I rap mostly, as this was my most preferred genre. It was there that I began to realize the potential that lies within me. "Your gifts and talents would continue to lie fallow if you are waiting for the right break, and when the right break comes, you might realize you were never ready". It became harder to cope in school, but I had high hopes for myself. School was not going to defeat me. When there was a need to do things, I gave it all my best, and when things were a bit less, I would take to all my endeavors – not a way I would prescribe everyone should live. It could have been quite better if I had people to help me with, but as I mentioned I had fewer friends than promised. I was not odd, I just didn't have people who share the same zeal. In my later years, I have seen people who are so bound with the need to have people in their life go for anyone available. This I can tell you this for sure: If you align yourself with someone who does not have the same zeal as you do, you both are headed for demise unless one of you decides to let his dream go. I met with AMG in DC. Now the building was elegant in its own glory. Walking into the edifice, I was wowed by his splendor; this was a place I would love to be. We walked across a row of rooms before we reached his office. As I stepped into his office, I saw a lot of records on the wall, there were several photos of him and other artists hanging on the wall. This I expected. After we went on the terms of my agreement, one of the managers that would be responsible for my signing and acceptance into the label stepped into the room. His walk into the room was true to his work, he was the serious type, sure need to be he was responsible for how far he could summon to the ranks by the nature of the artist he signs. With the help of the manager, he was convinced that I was a good fit for AMG, or so it seemed. I got a four-year deal with AMG or say the contract with them. I was appealed, this was a guy still in his early years, I was still in high school, and now I have a contract with AMG, it is quite unbelievable for someone of my age to attain this reach not to talk of someone of my stature – a guy you would describe as unserious, but I was serious with music. My journey with AMG began.

"DON'T SECOND GUESS JUST GO WITH YOUR GUT, YOU NEVER KNOW"

Eric Cominski Jr

Chapter 3

"NOTHING NEVER lasts", "there is an end for everything", those were the words that kept ringing in my head. The good times and the Bad, the fine and the ugly, they are all meant to come and go. End is inevitable. I have ever been an ultimate believer there is always an end, how soon it would come I did not know. "Valar Morghulis" which translates to "all men must die", one of my favorite lines in George Martin's Game of Throne, revealed an end that is inevitable for man – death. Though death might be the extreme end, nonetheless we all see various ends come each day: the sun going down, the leaves drying up…. Our recognition of the end that has come or will soon come can go a long way to help us live life the right way. And when the end does come, our innate abilities to embrace it is a true honor for the valor. I had begun a new life signing with AMG. Music had made a way for me. The faint smile that falls across my face in those days is still coming on this day as I remember how far I had come. I would still agree with my younger self that it was a big deal. It was a beginning of a strong career for me. It was a career path that reached out to my soul, how I wished I could stir this course without end. Music, at that time, was brooding with respect. People had realized the pain, the sorrow, the anger, the life, etc. that were embedded in its lyrics. Most have recognized with different genres and they lived it in their life. Music was revealed more and more in my daily life, and I could say this was one of the things that made music a great break for me at that time. Thus, I started rapping with AMG. The days were some of the best I had, they were never over – at least in my mind. I did my best to get along. And my personality was a blessing to me at this point. I had age by my side and I have learnt to respect, the two critical things I needed to show forth. Youth and Respect had never from time been on the same path. The few ones who tried to make them get along paid dearly for it and anybody who tries to make them get along will surely do. I would point out that I still had complacency hovering over my head, I kept my head down whenever I needed to. To me, it was about understanding the time and what time needs. There were times you need to show your vigor as a youth and some time you need to be dumb. "Being dumb is not a disease, it's a pathway to understanding", my mother once told me. And as I moved in my daily life, it became clear to me that I was different – I had opportunities that most people of my age didn't have. I had to tread carefully.

I had to get understanding without disgrace and give respect without stupidity. Above all, I still had to live to my dreams. To me this life was new, and it was real. It was not out of fantasies as other in my age gap lived. I was interacting with the hard-real-world every day, everything about me was evolving. I was growing faster than the norm would think I should. Being signed with AMG was going smoothly. I had all the help I needed, they were there for me – more than the usual kind for an artist. I felt a sense of respect whenever I was in the company of the musical crew. Respect, they say, is reciprocal, I would believe that was what they followed. I still met with my manager who brought me in. He was someone I deeply respected and appreciated his effort with me and his frankness was, without say, my greatest gain. I would go to him to ask questions and get advice, I needed it to not fault. To me, this [contract] was a must-not-miss shot for me. I was doing my best, but it was easier – I would think so – largely due to the fact that this [music] was my thing from scratch – I was deeply in love with music. I looked forward to the times I would spend in the studio. Those were the days that brought a smile that lasted weeks. Do you have days like this? It is very expedient for man, no matter which path we wish to take in life, that we have days that brings a smile to our faces. Days when the stress is joy and the end is not anticipated. Days when the world seems to all work in our favor. Days we feel on top of the world and can be everything we want to be. Days like this don't come too often. But we must consciously craft out these days for ourselves, so we could recall the memories and laugh out loud the joy of the past. Come to think of it, at home everything was improving. I had not been serious with my academics like most of my classmates, but I had a thing going on – a good thing. When my neighbors and the rest of the family got to know I was involved in music, they were contented with me. And everyone wanted to help. Right then I realized, if you have a good thing going on, people would come out. It is not uncommon for people to judge you, but when they see something great starting to bud out, they would gather around to be at your service. I was offered a lot of help. But I couldn't quite tell then if it was because I was had things going on or it was out of pity that I had too many things on my plate. People could be like that, right? With all the help I got from all sides, it was still a clear fact that I was not doing great at school. I believe they sympathized with me that I couldn't do everything and still be so great with school work. But that still didn't stop mom sometimes to remind me that I was sent to school to study, and how getting good grades could be a better part for me in the future.

I was also concerned with school, but I couldn't quite figure out how to work everything together. It later became clear to me some things were going to suffer, and I was ready to take that risk. One of my biggest fans in music was my Uncle, Cornell – uncle in the sense that he was my aunt husband. I grew to be fond of my uncle. He told me he liked my songs, but I had work to do to get better. My uncle loved the fact that his nephew, still in high school, has a contract with a label. Getting into a record label or a contract was hard. I didn't know then, I would find out in later years. But I had a contract in the most awesome way possible. My uncle was one of the men in my life, and his role would forever be appreciated, he understood me. He told me he would help me with my music. I wondered how such a grown man could understand me that much. I have seen a lot of grown-up men, who don't seem to get even the slightest bit of knowledge about young boys, but he did. He understands the rebellion I needed, the attention that I detest and the freedom I want. He was my guy. He was not the stern type, even though I believed he would have lived through the hard times – war, internal conflict. He did his best not to show it. Men of his age were usually indifferent towards the younger ones. If you see a grown up in those days, and you did just ask a question. They would bury you in so much history and regrets your ears would hurt. He wasn't. He kept most of his comments to himself, about how bad the government was and how corrupt workers were. He had a firm voice, deep and collected, and was never in a hurry. I couldn't quite tell why. It was not that he was old or so, he just was never in a rush, took his time to do everything. And for a guy like me who wants things to move very fast, I learnt that moving slow might even be a sign of strength rather than weakness. My aunt told me he had been like that since she met him. How possible? Sometimes it was too good to be true, how could a person be so calm? Maybe that was why he was a friend of mine. He was all I ever wanted from a friend, ready to listen and not judge. While writing, his calmness got me thinking. Why would a person be so calm in this life of rush? What happened? I looked inward to see if I could get the clue of what may or may not have happened? Then it hit me, I have also grown to be calm. I was calmer than my younger self. I had seen lots in life, and I was growing to be more receptive rather than aggressive. I have experienced the shadows that life can cast on a soul, and I have been humbled by it. And it is true, not everyone grows to be calm, but the ones who do are dubbed better. "With age comes responsibility and silence", a wise man once said.

Though my uncle was a tale that was too good to be true, he had this bad knack of busting out sometimes and when he does that which it might be a result of him being happy or sad. His kind of outburst sometimes could be unhealthy. Those who don't talk much can be exploding, I concur with that assessment. When it happens like that, he just continues to say things, like a bucket being emptied; you do not want to be there. He continues to unbolt his feelings. Not a sight to wish for. It happened a few times, but I could live with that; At times I felt he can be selfish also. My uncle was more of my best friend than a father to me and his feedbacks meant a lot to me. So, when I started at AMG and told him, he was joyous without bounds. He had wanted to do music also at a time. My days in AMG were going well, and I was informed that people were interested in me. It was a great feeling to become the center point of a new sensation. My time at AMG was rather successful, and upon discovering that there were enough people gunning for me, I knew I had to get their attention somehow. How often do you try to get people's attention? Or do you even try? I always do my best to get people's attention every opportunity I have, you may never know who might help you succeed. We all cannot tell what the other person is thinking, but if he goes on to reach out for our hand, we would be willing to help. If he wouldn't, we also couldn't do anything. So is getting people attention. It is reaching for their hand, letting them know you are available, and you need their help. I wanted to get their attention, but how? I try to learn the best way to go about this. What was I going to do? Lots of questions loading in my head. One that struck out was; "Which artist do you prefer more, those who write their music themselves or those who had it written for them?" I believe, and with lots of research, it was revealed that listeners, promoters, record producers almost everyone love to have an artist that writes their songs themselves.

This is not to say that they sometimes did not want an artist that does not write. But when I posed my question to AMG, who took me in, he said, "if you sing and you write you song yourself, there is no acting, it is real". And that I do agree with him. Seeing an artist that wrote the song by him or herself listening to how the song flows was a different experience and an art distinct from others who didn't. There is always a tell, that the song was coming from the heart. It took me time, but I knew I need to be different; "How do I start?" I was not a gifted writer this was clear from early school days composition, essays or any type of writing. I had rhymes but didn't have the idea of staying on subject. That night, I had an expository discussion with him about my music contract.

It was high time l let him know the complete story – incomplete story – he always wanted to know, and this was my sign of opening up to him. He was already aware that I had begun traveling to DC but he I have never the whole story. I explained to him the music contract I had with AMG and the terms of contract. He was always pleased and happy, to say the least, that his nephew still in high school, had a music career. And his enthusiasm for me would be – I believe – what prompted him to offer help to write songs for me. That was how my uncle began to write songs for me. I was a rapper and I had a ghost-writer, it was perfect for me. I felt my uncle was proud of the fact that he was included in my music. And he also didn't need to cover it as his pride showed forth whenever I got the record the songs he wrote. The attention I sought for, I certainly did get. But things were not perfect at school. Back in school, my studies suffered, books were far from my reach. To be frank, I can't really say why I didn't drop out then. It was clear I had no business in school; not my thing. But would it have been the best option for me? No, it wouldn't. I was still very young and unprepared. Saying I would leave school to focus on my side hustling, modeling and music would be immature. I still had years of education to reap from. I thank the heavens that I didn't even at one time thought of leaving school, but I believe if I had, I would have lot of people to talk lot of senses into me. When most of my teachers get to hear of my report; the modeling, music, they concluded that I had other things that made my day, they were right. To them I was grasping at a future that was not there, I was doing something good for myself. I later realized that they treated me more with frangibleness, I was brave. I still didn't help things, as I sort of threw their help out of the window – it was intentional though, but that was who I was. Underneath the boy who was responsible to get a modeling job and rap alongside was a man who wants to be free from the school system and thinks the teachers were in it all along to get him. Such a juvenile I was! I was present enough in class to answer my name on the roll call or answer the hatred that arose from being popular. With everything going on, I still was not a stickler for the rules; I mostly sought out for a way to bend the rules. And this gets me into trouble, I was familiar with getting into trouble, everyone at some point was aware of my cordiality with trouble. It was normal for a boy of my age and stature to get into trouble. How would I be known if I didn't? I wouldn't applaud my juvenility, but I understand why I behaved like that then. Although I had a music contract and a modeling job, I had to watch my back at school – the customary high school beef of the lucky guy.

The news of my music contract and modeling job was no secret, and I had grown enough customer bases for me selling candy, CDs and DVDs which were thriving. I knew at a point there would be some type of hatred, it was meant to be. Someone is sure to want what you have and hate you for it. I think it's like balance, with so much of good comes a corresponding amount of bad. If there was a little imbalance anywhere, then things might not seem to be true. And if you have a good thing going on, and got no one to hate you, then you don't have anything going on. To them [my antagonists], selling candy and DVDs was tolerable, but doing music and modeling was intolerable and it was many people that found out and it escalated all through my stay in school. It was at this point that I discovered what success did for you can be so destructive to other people. They would go out of their way to put your foot in the ditch. When it all started, it was meant to be a joke. But then it grew, with all our innocence, I realized we could be a pain in the ass if we wanted. It all began with this escapade of some other rap artist doing a "diss song about me". Now when someone calls you out, you should respond; that's the manly approach, as opposed to being prudent which is labelled to be cowardice and I also had a stature to maintain. I was already getting familiar with the music industry and I was gaining ground. And with my status, I had to make one back. So, I did. From there everybody wanted to rap against me, fight me, had to call me out, whatever it took for them to get in the spotlight. It was like they were already waiting to unleash hell on me. As I tell this story, I recall my tenderness turning hard. I was treated not like a young man but as a grown man – who does that? They were completely out for me. And I was not going to back down, not now not never. I was born to fight, I was born to win. I made many "diss songs". To be frank, it was kind of exciting, the blood was flowing. It was like a football march with no rules. I would bless this experience in later years. One of the diss songs that really hit hard was the song called "100 bars & runnin" after that song I got well known and then things started to get tense. All my diss songs was done by me. I told my uncle that it was my fight I must do it alone and he agreed. It was great, and the downside was that my community of loathers grew. I was the high school rapper who had a contract, does modeling, sells candy and DVDs and still has the entire community of loathers to deal with at school. Believe me, it was exhilarating. There were days I wanted it all to be gone, who wouldn't? I was not a subject of beef or the other. Not that I had a lot of friends before, but this was new to me, I couldn't handle it, I couldn't explain it. I just wished every day that thing would become better. I did my best to stay afloat the troubling waters.

I tried my best to stay out of trouble, but it always seems to be that trouble finds me first. With the lots I had to deal with, I was sure I was going to always be in trouble. It wasn't far from the truth as with time, the principal at my high school already had my mom on the speed dial; I couldn't quite explain to her, it all wasn't my fault. But how was I to explain, what was going on at school. And I know she would have responded that, "You should have acted the mature one". Easier said than done. I tried my best to listen to her words, but they [loathers] always get the better part of me. I learnt I had to deal with this myself. I stop trying to explain to her any time I was in trouble, and I started learning. When life teaches, we all should keep calm and listen, else we might never learn. And life lessons are only taught once. My mom was not the harsh type but was not interested in getting called into the office of the principal for how bad her son behaved. She for once told me that how good it would have been that one day, she would be called into the principal's office for better news than that of her son getting into trouble all the time. I did my all to keep my cool every time there was a need to blurt out amid my loathers. The truth is a man can only be that cool and not longer than that – I was also a young blood. As my life as a rapper progressed, my uncle became more involved in it. Every time we would meet, and I would tell him how much they loved what he wrote, he was happy. All this while, my uncle did not know the full story and that the label didn't either. Whenever uncle would write few rap lines for me, I would practice it in his front, and I would dwell on it until it became mine. "If you say the lie long enough you would believe it is the truth", this was my case. I rehearsed with the lines repeatedly until it sounded like mine. Recalling, what I did then, it all sounds funny. I am still happy that I didn't have regrets that I can't live with. Is it ever possible to live a life without regret? That would mean such an individual never made a bad decision, and that would be superficial. Regrets are not in our ability not to make bad decisions. It is in our ability to make out lessons out of these bad decisions. To grow out these decisions, then we would not regret our living. The last time I went to DC was when I had to record one of the songs my uncle wrote for me that was going on my demo. I asked my uncle to come because I wanted him to see what I been doing and to be a part of what I was doing to the fullest. He had always wanted to come along. When I told him, he felt elevated. He was like he had won a lottery as he continued beaming the entire night I told him – could be embarrassing for a man of his age to be beaming like that. Thus, we traveled to DC together had a long talk along the way. He appreciated the fact that I wanted him so involved.

I went on to tell him about how beautiful and elegant the Music Company was. He was happy for me and could not wait to see it he replied. Upon arriving at AMG Records, my uncle, agreed the sight was pleasing to the eye and all the while I was playing it cool. He was grinning with a smile at how beautiful the place I worked at was. Things have changed he commented, I played well but I could see through his act. I was sure something else was up with my uncle. I feared something bad might happen. We enter the doors that led into the main building. My uncle waited to take the breath of a beautiful edifice in, the main room that houses the reception stood tall and it was less busy on this day. A young lady who stood at the desk recognized me and I informed her that he was my guest. I led my uncle between the rows of the room that led to the studio where I performed. It was a big nice fancy studio with pictures of rap artists who came and gone and one artist that grab his eye was 2pac and Digital Underground. He went on about how wonderful the artist was or was it his rap songs – if you love rap songs and you don't love that of 2pac that would be criminal (personal perspectives). To be frank, I also feel a certain degree of prestige; to be in the recording in the same studio as 2pac. All this while, he was taking the expression in, I always knew he was an admirer of great designs. After spending enough time in walking from the entrance of the hall to the end where the studio was, as my uncle took his time to take it all in, we entered the studio. The studio was set enough for a performance to take place, everyone who needed to be there was. I always loved the studio myself, as it was spacious and not too many people were there, and there was that space of self-expression. As you would have envisioned, the booth where the artist performed has a glass door through which one could see through the artist inside, it was sound proof – everyone had to talk through the mic and a screen, so you could see each other. They were closing a session when we came in, so we waited. When the session was finished, I introduced my uncle, who by the way was beholding the elegance of the whole settings, to the crew. He was proud and as he hit it off with the entire crew, they seem to be convenient with him sitting with them. I had to record one of the songs my uncle wrote for me that was going on my demo. The crew as usual love my lines enough to give me well-bred remarks at the end. The session took like an hour, two or maybe longer or lesser, I could not remember. All the while I was inside the booth; my uncle went on with the appraisal for the record, the crew and finally went on to appraise himself. In discussing with the crew, he told them that he wrote the song for me. He [my uncle] told them how he had been writing the songs for me.

Everyone had always appreciated the fact that I had my own lines by myself and they gave me a sense of respect. When they knew where the lines were coming from, I knew they would be disappointed. My Uncle made this day bad, as he went on to tell them about all the people he raps with, basically making himself look like "the man". It was a disastrous moment for me. I had built a prestige for myself, and now it was going down the drain. When I finished my last take, I came out of the booth and there was my uncle still getting on with the crew, but the look on the AMG team was telling me something else, something bad had happened. I have been having this bad feeling since the moment we entered the studio, now it has happened. I could not quite figure out what had happened. After the chat, my uncle looked up, saw me and realized that the day was over. My uncle and I bid our farewells and took our leave; they appreciated him for coming and made a rather sarcastic expression about his coming shedding light on his nephew. On the way back home, it seems as if my uncle was trying to explain what was going on, now I did not know what had transpired between the AMG team and him. I would later find out when AMG called me asking why I didn't tell them. I didn't tell my uncle the complete story that the record was not aware he was the one writing for me and I didn't tell AMG either – it was my little secret. This is sure to be my fault but could as well be theirs. I was in high school, had a music contract and wrote my own songs. These should have brought some concern to the table, but it didn't. And note, I am not saying this it was their fault; I am just expressing my opinion. I did my best to explain to them so as not to look fraudulent and be guilty enough to be innocent. After a clear discussion with them, I would describe it as so if they got my point, they told me they would keep in touch with me. I never understood why my uncle did that, knowing fully well that if I made it big one day, I was going to take him along the joy ride. –He was going to share in the glory experience – because I had the image. I feel to this day he was trying to get his shot by saying he wrote my songs. His thinking was if they knew maybe they would sign me. Well that's how I felt anyway. Although I had plans, the ordeal at AMG was soon behind me. After a while, near the end of my contract, they called, and told me to meet with a guy named E bogie. He wanted me to make a 2-guy group with his son, kind of like a Chris Cross kind of group. We were down for it, but it took for me to move out my mom house drop out of High school and live in a house until I finish my first album (about 2 months). My mom wasn't having it, so we didn't do it. After the AMG thing happened I did a deal with Face-off Entertainment, which turned out to be a scam and took my money.

You would have wondered with all the knowledge I have acquired how possible, I could not tell for sure how it happened. But I was defrauded without any substance of evidence to prove with. They were there a time and the promise of heavens was singing to my ear, before you know it they were gone without a trace. Heavens knows that till this day, I still hurt. I was too prepared to be defrauded, but in this light, I was eager, not prepared. Being eager, I soon realized, was not the same as being prepared. I have seen in my interaction with people, that so many are eager to get the job done, but not many are prepared to do what it takes to get it done. So, I ask you, dear reader, are you eager or prepared? I acknowledge that this was, in fact, my handywork, as the situation of being out of high school and having a job with an Entertainment industry was fascinating, I forgot to do all my due diligence. Being deceived was not at the top of my list. But I learnt a valuable lesson which would go on to teach me in life that the truth you believe is as real as the information you have. So, I stop doing music full time and started back focusing on hustling. The thing was that I still had issues back home with everyone wanting my spot. I was working a 9 to 5 plus hustling and then dealing with beef with other guys it was stressful. I think my mom was fed up and just moved to Gates, NC. She moved there to get away, no one wanted to move there but after a while, everyone just dealt with it. I still had a year left to finish high school and a year left on my contract with AMG when mom decided to move to Gates County in NC. I would in later appreciate this move, as I have a lot of poisoned atmosphere in my high school. The move for me then was not welcomed, but now I can see what brilliancy the change has caused for me. My music life was at a stop, not everything last. I had more loathers than one can imagine, and I wasn't doing well in school. It was about time. At Gates County High, I met the best thing that ever happened to me, I met the love of my life.

*"LOVE IS WHAT IT IS DON'T USE OR WASTE IT,
ENJOY IT"*

Eric Cominski Jr

Chapter 4

AS I BEGAN TO WRITE this part, the radio seemed to get loud, it was a song I so much love, it was Ed Sheeran's Perfect, I couldn't help but sing along as it was the story I will tell, and thus I joined in:

"…I found a girl, beautiful and sweet

Oh, I never knew you were the someone waiting for me Because we were just kids when we fell in love…

…I found a woman, stronger than anyone I know

She shares my dreams, I hope that someday I'll share her home, I found a love, to carry more than just my secrets…"

I was lost in the words of this song before reality kicked. I had to continue telling…but it was also telling its part, it was already telling my story. I had to tune down the volume of the radio to tell my story. Smiles eluded my heart as I remembered those times. It was the time I fell in love. Though I had challenges to go through, I was still able to fall in love. Now I am asking myself, in the middle of everything that was happening you still fell in love, how come? I can't say, I can't explain love, but I know it happened to me while I was hustling. But love helped me, it kept me through. I thought back and realized it was true; times I needed someone to hold my hand when I need someone to cry on in my bad times. I have lived through these times not because I was very tough or so strong, but because I love. Have you ever loved or be loved? I am not a love expert, but my experience with the love of my life has taught me a great deal to withstand the stand of time with love. The feeling of loving and being loved, I can't describe, I can only say it is magical. Yeah, I believe it's magical, you can't say were the feelings stem from, the joy, the smiles, the satisfaction that meets your soul when the both of you meet. I could never explain, or can you?

I believe love is one of the things that is over human understanding, it was intentionally designed to be like that. But how did I get there? How did I fall in love? It all began like this: We had left Virginia during my last year in high school, it was a way for mom to escape my usual trouble. I sympathize with her. When we left, we moved to Gates County in North Carolina. She wanted to get a bigger house anyway so with all the mess I was in, it just gave her a push to do it faster. Gates County is a small rural area located in North Carolina and shares a boundary with Virginia – I was actually far from home. Like Trenton, it also got its name from General Horatio Gates, the commander of American forces at Battle of Saratogia – the decisive battle that led to the victory of the Americans over the British in the American Revolutionary War. Agriculture and forest products were its main industries. It was different from where I had lived, and it was a change I hated but then loved. I love to visit the Merchant Millpond State Park, it was a real beauty. The freshness was incomparable with the places I had visited then. Though it was not that I fell in love with the city, at first sight, I didn't. I was still angry at the fact that I had to leave Virginia – in my last year for Christ's sake. What was mom thinking? It was that anger that wouldn't allow me to see the beauty until a few weeks later. At former high school, Virginia, I did sports, Track & Field and Volleyball to be exact. Without any prejudice, I was good all of them. So, if you were wondering what I did for fun, that was it. It is necessary for everyone to have that hobby that helps you blow off steam. For me it was all of these sports. Right, I have heard people say sports was a waste of time, that having fun was not what life was meant for, you are meant to work. I have even been told at one time, "you rest when you are dead, work your ass off". I feared the person that told me that, but I do understand where he was coming from. I would tell you to work hard but have fun while at it. It is true, life is not a bed of roses, we must stand and fight, but what joy is there in fighting if not winning, and what way to celebrate winning if not have fun. Fun to me was not only a way to celebrate victory, but a way to retreat, regroup, and re-strategize. It was a "re" time for me, and it should be for everyone. Also, there is time for everything. A time to work and a time to play, a time to live and a time to rest… If you do not have fun when you can enjoy it, when are you going to? "There is a time, when you would have no joy in them". At a very young age, I had learnt the importance of time. Mastery of time was what all the great men use. When I was learning, I realized they had the same time and resources I had but what made them different from me was how they spent their time.

They understood that dimension of space we all clamor it was insufficient. If you understand the time, you would know when to stop working and have fun, and when to quit having fun and work. In school, I had always love P.E. [Physical Education], I was up and running whenever it was PE class. I couldn't quite say what got me so interested, but I am sure keeping myself fit was what I did best then, and PE promised that. My love for PE was very evident, I didn't give the coach handling it headaches. He was always surprised as I would see him smiling, a little bit disappointed. But it was not the subject, it was what the subject can do to me but that which it could do to my appearance. On getting to high school I did not relent; PE classes were the only ones that could call me calm. I tried enough to get better at all sports in high school. I am not the die-hard fan who can tell you all the mechanics and dynamics that went on in the game, but I was quite familiar with it. I went to games, which I might say was one of the things that fuel my passion for playing sports. I was a beloved fan of Allen Iverson and still am, I loved his style and how he had his game. There is something about him, I couldn't quite put my hand on, that made him different from the rest of the players. Anyone would believe with me that Iverson is a great player – you should check the basketball hall of fame, he is one of a kind basketball player, and he also began playing basketball while he was in high school. He also played football too. Then, I believe I could too. But I can't say now, I didn't go the basketball way. If I had would I have been great? I really can't say. Throughout my high school days in Virginia, I was in almost all games. This helped me with my skill. I could tell you for sure, that being great at sports and everything I got going made some people want to throw me off the cliff. It didn't even help on the pitch when I would become an example for the rest of the students. But I wasn't going to stop. No matter what I was facing, I was stubborn, I was not going to let down. I believe if you want something you go for it. That was what I did then. But I would advise you to never let your guard down, it would be disastrous. Some people are just waiting for that moment you would take the wrong step, and you might not make it back in one piece. In Gates County, there were about five schools; one high school, one middle school, and three elementary schools, aside from the Rosenwald Schools – such a small way of life. At Gates county high school, it was dawned on me that I had a year left to University. I had one year to prove myself good enough to be admitted into a good University. I had to give my all. But I was not going to stop my side hustling, I believe I could get into college with everything on my plates. I wasn't a geek or so, I just believe in myself.

To me, getting into the college was a matter of convincing the admission board than of being an exceptional student or so I was told, and I had a year to convince them. I knew right then, I had to focus on my strengths, which were PE and Mathematics. Focusing on my strength is one of the very many techniques I used all through my life. Anytime I need to do something, I would look at myself and gauge myself on the things I have that could help me get there, and then focus on the ones that are my best. Focusing is one way to go in life. And true, I might not be completely right, some people might not need to focus, they might be better if they diversify. Fine if you do. But still diversify in your strengths, not in your weakness. I knew what I wanted to go for, better-enough grades, and a convincing performance to get into a good university. I would describe this last year to be one of the serious years I had as a student, I would go on to have more serious years. Daily I leave for school and it was clear to me that each day brought me closer to the end of high school and the start of the college education. Even though I had this primal goal – getting into college, I still went about my daily hustling. I still sold candy, CDs, and DVDs, and I still had one year left on my contract with AMG, but I knew they would never call back after what happened. At Gates, I made new friends and I said to myself, "be out of sight", but somehow, I got back in the light and its Virginia over again. I was the new kid on the block, so some people like me, and some didn't. Gates was a small town, so word got around quick. The only difference was that it was not that much, and I handled it gracefully this time. The best thing that would happen to me at Gates was Casheem, the love of my life. I still smile as I remember those moments that brought us together. I was not the easiest to go around with, didn't have the best repertoire, but I still found something more precious. I couldn't quite believe myself on the day I beheld the one greatest thing in my life. I met this lady in one of the classes I took at Gates County High. She had an ebony-dark hair which flowed over her shoulders. Her face was radiant with the smile she always had on. Her voice was a sweet mellow to my ears. I took my time to study her like she was a class I took. Every day I looked forward to the class just to see her. And she was calm, she would just go on shifting her elegant gaze up and down the board. I couldn't stop seeing her, I couldn't get enough of her – believe me, it was not an obsession, I just was locked into her. We started out just looking at each other every day in the hallway as we walk past each other smiling at each other until one day I message her on Myspace. After then we met. It was like a slowed movie as I began to approach her.

And as I moved closer to her, she smelled of newly plucked rose, her fragrance was none that I had ever smelled – could be an overestimation, but I wouldn't mind. Her voice, when she began to speak, soothing to hear, I would beg the time to stop and return me over to them when I behold this Amazonian beauty. I believe I was lucky, not many people with my kind of lifestyle found love. But the fact that I did is evident that everyone can. I was someone who didn't have time for other – they mostly didn't have anything to offer, but I found time for this woman. This time had to be a little bit better, I told myself. Not only myself, but for my mom. I have done enough harm to my mom already, I should give her the peace she desires and more, so I should start thinking about college. The push I got from my girlfriend at this new school also went a long way to help me go through the storms. With love and school, I kept hustling. The days of hustling for me were not yet over. I still did enough hustling by the side to save up for the raining days. I had left my former job at Popeye when we left Virginia and I was able to join McDonalds when I arrived at Gates. I also got a temporary job at a warehouse in the County. And by now, I had known enough how to manage my time. Time was a servant I chose to master. I have seen many people, became servants to time, but I have learnt to own my time. I learn that to master time, you must clean up. There are lots of energy we spend daily that we shouldn't because those things we are using it for might not be. Cleaning up is very crucial to start mastering time. Then I would advise that anyone who wants to go on to the mastery of time should grow smart. Many people work, but few will work smarter. So, I chose to work smart and I can say with all the latitude of reality, I am a success. Casheem and I had a lot of things in common, and she was subtle enough I did my best not to lose her. The road of our love was rough, I still think it was meant to be like that, or who have you seen that didn't have a sad story to tell? When we started going out together, we would have arguments and take long before we reconcile. But we grew to the points when we sought it out in a jiffy. And whenever we had arguments like that, things become a little bit messed up which I didn't know at that time. But writing now, I can evidently tell my experiences. Love, at first sight, was what I had with her, and anytime we had arguments, things become muddled up – what love could do, huh? I could remember a time; we had an argument overnight about how I kept her waiting after school hours. I was certain it was my fault, I had to meet one of the teachers after classes and the meeting took longer than expected. She said I need to let her know not keep her waiting, and how I had been doing that lately.

All I needed to do was to say sorry, I wouldn't, and she disconnected the line. The next day I saw her, trying to behave like nothing happened, but something did happen as to how cold her response was to me, and I can remember all through that day. I felt terrible, my tummy felt strange all through – I would later know it was symptom of feel sorry for the one you love. And there were more experiences which are reserved for another day. Sorry, not a love story book. I graduated one year earlier than Casheem, at that time my girlfriend. So, I waited, I wanted us to move on together. I was not ready to leave her behind – I couldn't tell what would happen if I did. Yeah, love can make you do some crazy things because I am currently laughing as I am reminded of my decision then. And in that year, I did a lot of work, I grind hard – I was out of school, I've got all the time in the year. I worked hard to save enough for the both of us [me and my girlfriend]. I worked between the hours of 9 and 5 and would later worry about my side hustling. Still had my candy and CDs business going on, sales were coming. And you shouldn't also. You have one life to live, do not let anyone live it for you. If you would go on to mess it up, do so, it is your life. But that's not the point – messing your life up, the point is live your life with those decisions that came out of your bosom. And am also not saying you should listen to advice and opinions. Please do. What I am trying to get across at this point is that even though you listen to different opinions, you should fight through it – they are all offering their best, no one knows the best answer. Every decision you make is your burial, you should dig the grave. The idea of joining the Marines, maybe at that time was great, but makes me want to puke now. It would have been a disaster if I went on to join the Marines – I was never built for that kind of life, believe me. I canceled out the Marines and I was not able to find a college that would accommodate my life, so I focus on hustling and grinding. In the course of my search, I came across an online schooling. Yeah, online school. The Internet is great, bringing even the most sophisticated knowledge to our doorstep. Not long ago I was surfing through the internet and I came across so many courses that were offering master's degree online – it could be that easy, I just smiled – it was for people like me. I went to online school at DeVry for Computer information and Business as a full-time student and I worked two jobs. And then I tried to get back into music, but it wasn't the same. I wouldn't say my zeal had gone, but that it had grown out of me. Don't get me wrong, I still love music, but the zeal I had in my earlier days were diminishing, I couldn't say what caused it. But at that time, music was not what I wanted to be doing. What I wanted more was to get out to the world.

After the incident with my uncle at AMG, we were at odds for a while. I couldn't understand why he did that. Now, I believe my anger towards him was juvenile. He didn't mean harm to me. It was a mistake. Well I hope it was but it's a thing of the past now. The fall out with my uncle wasn't long. I was back interacting with. While I spent time with him he introduces me to a guy who would later become a very good friend of mine. His name was DOT R. My uncle was working on building his own label and was working with DOT R. He got me along with this guy, and I enjoyed his company. He didn't have a stench for indifference, but all the same, he made his grounds known. I respected him. Even though we had moved to Gates County, our house was getting full. I was now living with my mom, my stepdad, my grandma, and two of my sisters with their kids. I had to get out of there. I didn't mean to be rebellious or classy, but I needed space – I am sure you get it. At a certain time in our life, we want space, and we must have it. Those who don't lose themselves. Why do we need this space badly? I believe, we need it to grow. That's is why we should understand it when someone tells us he or she needs space. Our ability to grow is what makes us human. Let us grow and we live on, don't let us and we die – so is every human being on the planet. So, after much discussion with my mom, I planned to move out. But would not until after Casheem got out of school, then we use the money we had saved up to move out together. I needed space to grow and I found space to grow with my love.

"THE ONLY PERSON HOLDING YOU BACK IS YOU, STOP BLAMING OTHER PEOPLE"

Eric Cominski Jr

Chapter 5

IT WAS JACK MA'S life that I saw at this point. As I began to pen down those days, I realized how true his [Jack Ma] foretold mine. It foretells how I started. "We will make it because we are young, and we never, never give up", those were his words when he started Alibaba. And today, he is about the second richest man in China. But his beginnings were never like that. Aside from the fact that he came from a poor background and didn't get the education he so much desired. He encountered rejections from schools and jobs he applied to. He also failed many times until he finally got it right. I looked back and realized that was me. I had seen this kind of zeal years ago. I smiled and continued. Jack was a revelation that at the end of every struggle, there is hope. Though I didn't know Jack when I started out, his ways were a sooth to me now and I remembered how far I have come and how far I still can go. One thing he emphasized most was the dream; people follow dreams, and money follows people. It is a thing of my mind. I had been using this method a long time ago, I had been following my dream. We moved to Newport News in Virginia, me and Casheem moved with some roommates. Both sides of our family didn't like the idea of us having roommates, but it was mainly to help us with bills and save money. It was a nice town house in a good-looking area that had a local beach about ten minutes away. We lived right off the main road, so it was a busy area also. When we moved we were excited, I mean who wouldn't be, but the only worry I had was our roommates holding up their end, so I would be able to get things going with my business with the extra money I would have. Newport News is a city on the James River in coastal Virginia. Downtown, the Mariners' Museum chronicles centuries of maritime history with ship models, figureheads, artifacts and a replica of the Civil War ironclad warship USS Monitor. The Virginia War Museum explores American military history. The Virginia Living Museum showcases local wildlife, including bald eagles and red wolves. When my girlfriend and I finally concluded to move to Newport News it was received with mixed feelings. But it felt like the right choice then – was it? I can't say. I told myself I was making the right choice and my girlfriend was with me – and if she was with me then definitely I was on the right track, right? Our families were very happy we took this step in our life. It really took a toll on me and Casheem.

We both went to school and was working full time jobs. On top of me trying to start my business off right. We pushed each other to our limits and then pushed some more. Together we were able to do anything. Do not take your eyes off the target. Some people took their eyes off the target, and they were long gone before they knew they had missed the way. It is not how tough you are but how much you can wait, persevere and do. Someone once said, "Everything you do should bring you one step closer to your dreams". We are meant to be consistent, and consistency brings out results because consistency itself is the end we all want. If we would put in more work, little effort, give ourselves small push in the right direction, we would someday reach the goal, it might just take time. And it really should. But while not taking our eyes off the target, we should not be spent out. There are a lot of energies in the body of a young mind, and his or her ability to expend this energy is one of his greatest strength. It is not bad to want to use your strength. But I have seen so many spend their energy in ways they can't even say it would affect or take them towards their dream. They had too many things to do, so many places to go to, lots of people to attend to...and at the end of the day, they were spent and have little to show for their journey towards their dream. They couldn't cut. They couldn't say no. They couldn't resist. But, what if I told you that cutting is one of the best ways to gaining, huh? You don't believe? I have experienced cuts in my life – some I did to myself, others I didn't – and I have brought great gains out of it – not all though. Those cuts at that time also were not the sweetest choices to pick, I wouldn't want to leave music for a while, I wouldn't want to reduce my time with sports …but I had to. I would bring more fruits to myself if I bear with the less I had. I would be better if I could cut back on most and focus on a few. Please do get what I am saying. "Life would come and go, and it has lots of offerings to offer, our ability to be successful is not how full our plates are but how full it can get after we have sowed and harvested". The fortitude of life is not in many, it is in the brave ones that count as hundreds on completion. And our strength is mostly shown in our ability to cut. The cutting of excess from the garden flower brings out its beauty. Look around you, what things do you need to cut? It's never too late – at least not until you are dead. My girl and I did our best to cut on our spending. We were cutting through anything that was possible to cut: parties, celebrations, exotic shopping, etc. If I wanted to take my girl out, I had to work extra hours. This day I would remember those times and joy would fill my heart. I still remember the pain it took, the sadness I had to endure sometimes.

But at the end, the beauty of my butterfly had struggles and its wings tell of its gloriousness. And I think it was this – cutting and focusing – that made us move in silent mode. We had a lot on our plates, we were different. Believe you me it is great to be different. We moved with confidence that we are having a future we saw together. What can the power of seeing the future do to you? When I saw the future that I wanted to achieve, I had to change my mindset. Your mind is the most powerful influence on you – take it or leave it, that's the radical truth. With your mind you believe, you imagine, you create…it's the powerhouse that reinforces you. It is the master. Do you want to change something? Change your mindset. Do you want to get somewhere? Change your mindset. Do you want to be somebody? Change your mindset. Let your mind go before you. Our mind is that big factory where the next big change would come from. Ever heard of the saying "we are the product of what we think" or "What you think is what you imagine, and what you imagine is what do and what you do is what becomes of you". Yeah, I do listen to lots of inspirational and motivational speech – and you should too. They keep me at bay. The greatest strength of a man is his mind. Control the man, control the mind. I would forever emphasize the need to change one's mind to everyone I would interact with. The first question I pose to anyone that seems to be needing my help is; what's your mindset towards what you want to do? But for me then, I knew what I need to do. I need to change my mindset. I had to change my mindset to grind mode – Work! Work! Work! Work! Work! like Rhianna sang. I had to switch to grind mode. I had to convince myself that I was not like other people and would not grow on to become another if not myself. The reins to me were clear. Though I know I couldn't do music in full time as I wanted to, I can't still accommodate. My decision to cut made me see a path – one of the pluses of doing the cutting. What could I do with the little time I have to spare for music? What? And the idea of doing battle raps hit me. I have always preferred rap to all other genres of music, so it was not going to be a hard work for me. Most of us if we do listen – it would be weird if you don't – to music should be familiar with rap, the genre of music where you have to muster words fast enough to fall in line with the beat and still dwell on the melody of the song. Battle rap is a special case of rapping in which the persons involved, mostly two people, are rapping in an argumentative manner each trying to prove its point. There are audiences that love to be involved in this type of scenario. Most of the battle rap I went to would start on the note of someone picking on the subject of discussion.

At these raps, not all of them are argumentative in nature, some are about a subject matter which you try to make points as clear as possible, some are about your fellow rapper – trying to diminish something about him and at other times, it is just berating some system. In the end, your aim is to make your opponent feel bad, only a winner must emerge, that's why it is called battle rap. But when did it all begin? It all started in the year 1981 between Kool Moe Dee and Busy Bee who would go on to begin the revolution in rap known as Battle Rap. They faced off for an 8-Mile-style contest, two fearless rappers. But Kool Moe Dee won because he made a meat loft out of Busy Bee who was busying entertaining the audience. And from then on, we would go on to have better and gruesome rap battle down the drain. One that really did make history and was known very well – probably because they both are gone now, was the one between 2pac [Tupac Shakur] and Biggie. It was different in so many ways they both applied their signature to the raps. 2pac kept on his insults as explicit and aggressive – which is not unusual, and Biggie gave subtle insults that were delivered with ease as if they weren't what they were – insults. This rap battle would go on to change history, as it affects the entire region, changed lives and destroyed relationships. What battle rap could do... But aside from the blood fact. It can be great. I believe battle raps teaches one about the mastery of words in limited time while thinking about the future. It was a way to get out of your end and into the game, a way to dwell on someone else's weakness while preserving your strength. You could be all out, or you could be all in. Not everyone would come across these scenarios in life, and the lessons these scenarios teach us is undefinably great. But if you have ever been in an argument – please tell me you have, that would mean you have been under pressure to reason and act to get your point across. Battle rap is a glorified kind of argument. But like every situation is not for you. You can never be good at all. I would later realize that battle rap was not a show of my elegance. Things would not always go as planned. I thought battle rapping would be a way to situate myself better to the rays of the entertainment industry, but I was wrong. How many times have you been wrong? For me, lots of time. If you ever tried, you could be wrong or right, but if you never tried, you may never know. That was one of my first lessons in failure. I wouldn't be able to tell someone that battle rap wasn't my thing if I hadn't tried. Yeah, I was a good rapper, but I was not good with battle raps. We would come to this later. After few battles, things began to go awry. Be reminded, I was not a fluke at this. I had done diss before, just that this was a lot more proclaimed and insulting than dissing.

I won some battle which some would describe at been too good to be true, and some that I lost because I was still human. I have experienced it. Some battle raps where both players turn to go for blood, it can be bloody. I just wondered how everything could be the same after they were through. No matter how much I had to say against my opponent, I still kept a sense of humanity in it. I believe words, when spoken can never be taken back. And they [everyone] would use it on you when they need to, you should mind how you use your words. Outside of rapping, I did little of talking. I had learned that out of 100 things you have to say, you should carefully choose only 10. I believe this 10 you say are the best of it, and if when crafted they can last longer and not only for you but for others as well. People can remember lots of words, but if you want to get a message across you've got to use few words; few words that prick the heart and startle the mind of men! Words will all stand the test of time. The more you say the lesser the reception, the less the better. Few words are better, fewer words are the best. At some point in my battle career, my opponents were no-show. I always wondered was I on fire or I was never on fire. Things can be blurring at this point. It happened a few more times before I came to the sensation that something was going on. When an opponent of mine was no show, I was angry. And most of the times, it was my opponents that would propose the battle, I wouldn't. I had begun to be taking men words with lesser gravity, which would go on to influence my life. While I was battling the question of why people were no show to my battles, a report was going around how I was not a real battle rapper, or I was too good to be fought against, which one I couldn't quite recall. All I can say is I also knew I was not meant for this part in life, I was not bloody. When I started battle rapping, I started it has a way to have fun and mess around a little. But as I began to grow, things began to change, it was quite different from the diss I had in high school. It was getting farther than I could control. Some insults sometimes were so uncivil it knew no boundaries. It was without boundary and I wasn't built for a life without a clear distinction between the go and no-go area, I had to stop. Thus, my moment as a battle rapper was short-lived, this I would not have envisioned. For me, it was a moment of realization. This is a very critical point in one's life when we come to the realization of what we have within and use it to judge or quantify what we are giving outside. We all try to be things we are not, we try to be we think we should but at the end, it would be best for us to come to the realization that not everything we think we should be we have the capacity to be.

And most of the times, when we focus on things we think we should be, we lose the things we are and can be. At other times, there might be a conflict in things we are and things we think we might mean and we expend all our energy trying on conflict resolution. But if we know, we can spend less worry about the inevitable dissatisfaction that may come on us. I came to this moment, though I was a rapper, I could flow with lines without obstruction, I could use any subject matter, the words were there. But at the end, I was not built to be a battle rapper. I was not bloody, I was great at rapping but bad at battling. I could only be grateful for this earliest realization of mine. Better late than never, right?

Thus, I stopped battle rapping. However I had to focus on the rest of my side hustling to get through the times. It was not until I started living on my own, did I realize the pain that goes with it. But I wasn't unprepared, life had taught me a lot to live on my own. I had started learning at a young age, and they came in very handy when I needed them the most. I had bills and rent to attend to, the principal determinant of a reliable shelter. I would look back and realize what a young responsible man, I had made out of myself. I would realize the extent of my growth and smile at the progress I had made over the years. Looking back is a way to gauge your present and appreciate your past. I do almost all the time look back to understand some choices I had made, appreciate it and at other times berate it. Our ability to not lose sight of the history is one of life greatest gift to us. When we begin to forget our past, mistakes we made years ago are bound to repeat itself. And I wouldn't say we should live in the past, God forbid, we should live in the present. But our celebration of the past at more times than none gives us the hope for the future. I had mentioned before that when my girlfriend (my future wife) moved into the new apartment we had roommates, this was to help us divide the load equally, and it was a fair deal. I stood by mine, theirs was another story. How could I have known? I had begun investing myself into building my business. I had a great tale in mind, I was gathering enough information to make the business worthwhile; it is going to be great for me. I was going to be successful. But wait for all these plans without a fluke? Yes, as you would have envisioned, something was not going to go as planned. Every story must have some twist, right? How we want life to be without a twist. How we desired that life can be a journey no bumps met. How we wish. But is it not life? Our wishes are far from what we get. So was mine. If you could tell at every moment in your life what would happen, what wouldn't our life be?

If you could tell the rain is going to fall, you would take the umbrella or if you knew that the market was to crash in weeks to come, you would start clearing your account. But the ability to not know all is definitive for the possibilities of making mistakes and the possibilities of making mistakes is being human. To err is human, to forgive is divine. I had made a mistake which fayed itself as a great plan; I had built castles in the air thinking I had a solid foundation. My mistakes were with my roommates. After a month, my roommates were not paying their half of any bill I was left to cover everything. This was another one of the experiences that made me realize how gullible one can be when you need help and how people can be when they have gotten it. I have started to see first-hand, how people would go on to disappoint you without just cause, or a befitting explanation. It was really disturbing. I can still sense a repugnant feeling within me as I remembered those moments. It was a help that turned to hurt. It was when I realize you could trust people as far as their word go. I would still see them [my roommates] later in life, but that stain is forever there. That is why I advise everyone I see do you best to not hurt others, it would forever leave a mark that may never be forgotten. With my roommates, I believe I would have made a better choice if I had known. The if I had known speech… If I could tell at my first encounter with them, I would have, but I couldn't, or can you tell from someone's look that they would hold their end of the bargain. It was true, I had a rather successful life managing the first half of the bill, but that was not a determinant for them to act otherwise. We had a deal. From when life starts to when it ends, deals will be made. Trust will be broken. Contract will be violated. That's the way of life. Our abilities to live above whatever outcome that seems to appear is not a function of our environment but more of our innate strength. And I didn't say because I was faulted on this deal, I would not go on to make deals anymore. I would go on to make some great deals in life that have made my world. I just learn from every deal I made. And to that point, this would be the second bad deal I made, the first was with the Face-off entertainment scam, do you still remember? Even though

I tried my best to get the best roommates. My best was not enough. But I have stress to blame if I was going to play the blame game. If you live in the same county as the one you want to find accommodation there is lesser stress, but I live in another city. I was coming from Gates County and going to Newport News. I made trips back and forth the way. And on getting to this new area, it is not as if there are empty houses lying around waiting to be occupied, you have to source for it. You could contact the housing agency, but that at a reasonable amount, I could not afford that. So, I had to do the finding myself, in the process of finding, I had to take into consideration the easy to which to move between places I would want to spend my time. After getting one place or two, I had to bargain the price down because most of the houses I found were beyond my reasonable payday. I searched through and through until I arrived at one apartment which was the perfect location. I wanted this house so much not for its perfectness but also the price was considerably moderate. The price was agreed on and I took on the house. But I could have a better way with this, I could have roommates. Having a roommate, as I asked around, was not meant to be a big deal, just that everyone should get in touch and agreed on something. How bad can it be? So, I went for the option and contact few guys who wanted to be my roommates. I just asked them a few random questions, it was never meant to be an intimate thing, just looking for someone to stay in the same building and share the bills and rent. After my encounter with them, I contacted them, and they were in. There was absolutely no need for any due diligence. That was how I met myself in this predicament. This is not to say that I justified my actions, I should be rebuked for them. I had made all those decisions at the heat of the moment. I had a nice place and I had people who wanted to become my roommates and we were all students. And that would be my card if I were to play the blame game…but I wasn't. I had made a mistake, I am going to own it. Do you also own your mistakes? When I was a bit younger

– before this point in my life, I was taught to own my mistakes because I made them. Yeah, there are a lot of things to blame for it, but owning your mistakes is not about being weak it about being strong. It is not that you are giving a way for people to come at you – let them come if they would, it is just that you are growing in the way that you love to live or die, I would live life for myself. Till today, I still go about telling my folks to own their mistakes. Right from that point that you realize you had made it. Own it, damn it! It's your mistake, who else better to own it than you. But that shouldn't be a space to grow in making so many mistakes, got it? Making the same mistakes over again is outrageous. You've probably heard of the saying, "it is a madman, that does the same thing over and over again expecting a different result", so also it applies to mistakes. Still, I wished…If I could turn the time backward, I might make different choices. Then another question popped up in my heart, is making a different choice definitive for a better outcome? How can one tell of the best choice to make? Had I researched on them, would I still not come to the same conclusion? Had I moved on to the next persons, would they hold on their part of the deal?

All of these is telling us one thing; you can never be too careful, events will come – unplanned for, unprepared for, unwelcoming, but the events are not what matters, your response to these events is what counts. When it finally dawned on me that my roommates were not going to play their part, I had to respond well. At the end I let them stay and chose to cover everything. A deliberate act of maturity. Why choose to cover everything? At a point in our life, we would all look back. We would either smile or be sad. I believe we would be bound to smile if we were the reasons for others to smile; and we are bound to be sad if we cause sadness in others. Be the light in another person's darkness. I adapted to what happened and changed my mindset on what needed to be done. I put my business on hold to grind and hustle to keep bills paid. I had the means to cover everything; I just had to make some sacrifices along the way. And I was also graced to cover everything just that my business had to be on the hold. All my earnings were saved; every ounce of trade I made was saved to cover the entire bills. I had to come to myself that they would be gone when things were dawn on them or is it that I prayed that they were gone, I can't say. And my prayers were answered… After a couple of months, the roommates left, and it was just my girlfriend and me. When they announced their departure, joy eluded me, I did my best to contain it, but I couldn't. It was going to be great for me. I wished them well wherever they were going. When they [roommates] had left, my girl and I had the place to ourselves. But not until after 6 months did we realize that at this rate I would never get my business off the ground, so we end up moving out to a cheaper place. I told my girlfriend it's not because we couldn't afford it, it's because I have better plans for us. I'm aware of what I am capable of and where we were at was helping us grow. We had to downgrade where we lived so I could upgrade our future. I had to change my mindset. I adapted, and then I executed. It was one thing for you to say or plan something but when you must do it, it is really tough, believe me. As I look back at these moments I discovered my values were part of the reason I kept going. It had been what has distinguished me from others. What are your values? Values they say are embodied in our nature. They come out in due time, anytime we go through some change. It is our values that determine which path we take next. And today, the question that bothers me most is not 'do we have values?', rather it is 'Do we have the right Values?' Great strength, gifts, talent without the right values will falter in time. What do you Value? For me, I have seven things I value, number one is my time. Time, I cannot get back, so I value my time over everything.

I was young when I began to learn about the value of time. When I read about those who had made it, how they had worked and the things they did, I discovered that they understood the best use of their time.

They understood Time. They valued Time. Number two is my family, I love and care very much for my family. The fabric that binds us together as a family –blood – is not one we can ever severe. We can severe bindings by class, race, sex, religion…but bindings by blood can never be. And appreciating these can go a long way to prevent our past from going into extinction. Not only time, I believe family is the best thing that can ever happen to you. Number three is knowledge, the more you know the more you can do, and easier life gets. But someone still points out that with more knowledge comes greater sorrow, I would realize this in later life. Knowing would ever be an essential part in the life of a man who wants to grow. Knowledge is what we should all value, we should sort and search for it with every drop of sweat we have. "In all thy getting, get wisdom". My health is the next thing I value. If I can't take care of myself I can't be here to be great. If by tomorrow, I fall and go on to the beyond, life would move forward, Health they say is wealth and I valued it. Though I was hustling now and then I kept reminding myself of the importance of a great health. Value your health, no one would live this life for you. I also do value morals. It has been important to me to always if I can, do what is right. If our society weren't governed by morals, we would be a bunch of radicals roaming the streets of the earth. I believe morals are what gave us the decency we have over cannibals, it is what differentiates us as the human race. It is our indwelling on morals that makes the day bring meaning to us. Legacy, I so much value my legacy. I value what I was doing with my life; and so much more, I valued what I would leave behind. Or do you not think about it? About what would happen when you are gone? When you can no more answer to your name? It gives me chill to think about it. It makes me scarier to have the thought that after I am gone, the things that would respond or show forth my works would not be worth me. So, I strive every day to leave on a better legacy. The thoughts of my family also drive me daily to want to leave something for them. I want to build a lasting legacy. A feature I believe everyone should try. I want people to remember me forever and I want to live through my kids and those after them, and those after them… And I also value my brand and my business and what I do. If I didn't, who would? I had to value what I did so people could value it with me. Lastly, money, we need it for almost everything so it's a must to value my money and how I use it. Our world as humans is driven by money.

But very few people value it – these I have seen, and you cannot get the best out of something if you don't value it. All seven of these things I value and their realizations help me change my mindset focusing on the big picture and the main goal. Understand, know what needs to be done, change your mindset, and then execute. You might not get it right or find out what works, but you would never know until you try so the key isn't doing it right, it's doing it now. So, then we [my girlfriend and I] moved out to own place in Portsmouth, Virginia. Portsmouth is a city located in the Commonwealth of Virginia was founded by William Carwford who serve at the Virginia House of Burgesses. Portsmouth came into being as a town in the 1752 act of the House of Burgesses and since then it has been a well of history to the American States. The climates are such that one would enjoy outdoor activities all around the year – not like where I was coming from. The weather there is soothing to the skin; temperate and seasonal. Summers are hot and humid, while springs are wet. I would grow to love this town more. I just didn't come across it. I did a lot of searching – soul searching included, I just didn't consult read the stars, when I was looking for a place for us. It had to be a place that would accommodate us and let us grow our dream. We had to find that one place that would boom with the slightest spark. We may not always find that place, our utopia, but we can try, or as I have done, we can build one for ourselves. Searching for the perfect spot is never easy, but you can make the imperfect spot perfect. Those are the things we should strive towards. Not the imperfection that reins in the veins do we speak of but that perfection that is a product of imperfection is what we can achieve. We were going to make the best out of this new place. I would in later years call this place my Ebenezer. At Portsmouth, I found a good paying job and my wife did hairstyling. It was not going to be easy we were very sure of that. I believe this; if people deceive you, or you deceive others you should never deceive yourself. We didn't for once – when we moved to Portsmouth – we were clear of hardships. We knew the situation without our roommates was just the tip of the iceberg. We knew that we would go on to be disappointed, rejected, faulted, insulted…but we believe we shall overcome. Thus, we started our life. I was still doing my side hustling, going through online schooling and had a job. I had to figure out how to make time for everything, and about all, I had to figure out how to make time for us [my girlfriend and I]. Many I have seen complained of not having enough time on their hand to do something. The truth is you will never have enough time. If the thing you want to do matters, you would find the time. Plain and simple.

Then, my time was filled up I could not even enjoy life. I couldn't live life to the fullest, not because life was unfair, but because I planned to occupy myself so much living became an obligation rather than a life. I was stuck in the household of hustling. I am not saying that one should not work harder than others. You should. As a matter of fact, if you want to be greater than others, you have to put in more work than they do. But at the end of the day what matters to you is not how much you have spent, it is in how much you have brought forward. And mostly when we lose ourselves in working for ourselves – always grinding – we bring nothing forward; not talking about money or gain, but your time, your life, living to help others is the greatest gain for man. Planting in the human mind is the greatest gift of all. We [my girl and I] were growing and moving. Things were not going smoothly. It was hard. But we were putting in our best, after-a-while things were getting easier. We were learning, loving each other and working our asses out. This little light of mine, I am going to let it shine and go places with it. I would get jobs occasionally to get more to come in. I would volunteer at the first request to live a better life. It would all tell in my interaction later in life. After about 2 to 3 years in our own place, we got married and had our first son. It was a beautiful moment; the drapes were dripping, and the music played softly. We were going to be one. As long as I live, that moment she said, "I do", my world felt complete. She is the sweetest thing I've ever known. When our son came, I knew I had to do everything more. The time has come to step up my hustle. I had one more beautiful soul to work for, I had one more life to carry. I had to step up my hustle. It was the point of more responsibility; I was responsible for one more life than my wife and mine. And my son was perfect, I want to give him the best of the future he can ever have. So, I need to be more. To give more, I had to be more. I had to do more, not only that I had, I wanted to do more. I believe our wants and our needs they both align towards a better future. If what you want to do is what you need to do, then the world will sing of your praise from the hilltops. I wanted more, and I needed more for my family. I had to be a "real" entrepreneur – all my side hustling was not big yet, as I wanted it to be. Earlier, I had to drop out of school my grades started to slip after a while so dropping out was for the best. Dropping out of school as being kind of a signature for most entrepreneurs, right? Yes, but it is not due to the fact that we are tired of schooling, far from it, it is mostly due to the fact that our business is taking too much from us that we would have graduated as a fluke.

    Even though half bread is better than none, we, entrepreneurs, who have a budding business right from college, would prefer to put all our energy in either of school or the business. We could still come back for the degree. I shook my feet and bid school bye – for a while or forever I never knew. I was going to devote all my time to making my business known. I did research on starting a business and started to move on it with getting my LLC, EIN, permits, etc. I reached out to people to see if they would want to be part of or help with the idea. Everyone was down with it but when it came time for putting in work or money no one did. I ask my close friend, DOT R, my mom, my sister, my wife. The only two that was down from the start was my mom and my wife (DOT R came around later). I started to save money to have enough to start up with all the paperwork and legal stuff done. What's wrong with people? Any ideas? The first minute, they want to be the part you can't separate them from it. The next minute, they cannot be available. I had started something good, what they could just do to help was lend a hand. But they were too busy. Right then, I realize no matter how great you are or are going to be, people would not be out from the start, maybe they would come along the way. But when you start it you and only you alone and your family – that's if you have no friction with them. I ask many of my friends at work, people I grew up with, people I just meet, long life friends and no one really trying to do anything as far as putting up money or time. I made a promise to myself, that in later years when people call out for help. I was going to do everything in my power to get it. Starting a family was tough, starting a business was tougher and they were no one to help me. I felt so helpless I wanted to give up. It still saddens my heart as I am writing about this experience; I was still new, but no one came forward. Was I that bad? I always thought people didn't come because I was sort of different, or that they didn't understand. My wife and my mom were the ones there for me from the start. I can't still put my head around what would have happened if I didn't have them to tell me to go on. When dark moments come to one's life, having someone to call out to might be the fuel your soul needs. And at other times, it might not be that you need someone, it might be a word or set of words, or it might be some actions…there is just something to call us out in the dark. Even with these, there some people that refuse to be helped. They expected help from a source, but when they could not get, they refused help from all source – a great way to an abrupt end. So, it is not that we should have something to call out to us alone, but that we should be willing to receive it. Mom helped me with the finances, I wasn't so big on them yet. She gave me about five hundred dollars when I started up the business. And gave her unending prayers with it. I would bless that day every day till the end of time. What business was I into? I began my clothing line business. What? That is not anywhere near all I have been doing before. Yeah, I knew, I was also surprised when the idea hit me. But it was a wonderful idea. I was open to all ideas when I wanted to start my business and I would believe that was what helped me to make the best decisions. I have seen many people who want to discuss business ideas and are stuck with a particular sector in life. "All I want is an idea in the finance industry", they would tell me. I am sure most are afraid to do other things than those they are familiar with, but we all have to learn. If you want to do something, no matter the sphere in life, if you can learn, you have a shot at success. Great ideas that come your way may not be in your comfort zone; they would well be out of it. But learning and building is the way to grow. Yeah, I got the idea from a guy – I don't even know his name, but I would ever be grateful – at a battle rap event. Right, good things do come out of the bad. Battle rap wasn't my thing, but from there I got what I wanted. Such an irony in life! Out of the bad in our life, the best might come out. I got the idea for starting my clothing line at a Battle rap event when a guy came up to me and ask about my T-shirt. It was something I put together, a custom shirt that said Battle King on it. He asked, "is this from your own clothing line?" I replied and said, "No, it is just a shirt I made". I couldn't take him seriously more than that, why would one think a custom-made shirt is from a clothing line? Then he said, "You should probably start your clothing line, this looks nice". Wow, I could have figured out that one myself. And right there the idea hit me and that was what I was going to do. I was going to start a clothing line. To this day I never knew who that guy was that gave me the idea. And so, my world began. I was going to start a clothing line and fair enough I would use the name that the guy saw and appreciated, the name of the clothing line would be Battle King Gear. Thus, I got started. After getting everything started and getting products made; hats, shirts, jackets, and hoodies. It was not so easy, but I went on strong on, no one was going to stop me, and I wasn't going to stop myself. I did all the getting and managing myself. I wanted to get it out to the world at its best and I put in my all. But things did suffer, my time with my family – we would later discuss this. When I had got the necessary details and items I need to kick start my business, I went to everyone I knew to talk about starting the business with me. I wanted to see if I showed them what I was doing they would want to come along. I felt they thought I was joking when I met them and told them I wanted to start a business. That after seeing what I was doing, then everyone would join me. Or so I thought, as I got an entirely different reception from them. I was more than disturbed, why again? Everyone started to state how they wanted to start their own clothing line a long time ago and how they had the idea first. This was rather annoying even for those who seem very close to me. Why would they be like that? They could not be happy for me, why? It seemed no one wanted to support or be a part of the brand. They had the idea in their head, but why would that be a problem? Some even went to the extent of saying that I had made the brand about myself and so they couldn't be part of it. Wait a minute, was it not about myself? It was me from the start. I had the idea? Why should it not be about me? I could not understand as I came to everyone before I started and wanted them to be a part of it, but no one gave or brought nothing to the table so how was I making it about me? It had been me all the time. There was no need to make it about me because it was me already. I would later realize that man's ego to lay down his dreams for another is one out of a million. What I was asking then was that they would lay down their dreams to take on mine – which would have been selfless. But human would always be human, we would always find it difficult to lay down ours for the sake of others. Those who did, I would always salute. To me then, I counted it as sentiment. I just ignored the sentiment, focused on my grinding and I hustle harder, I going to take this thing to the next level. I now know I am the only one running this race, no help would magically come from anywhere, I had to motivate myself, drive myself, help myself…and so I began.

"DON'T MATTER WHAT YOU DO, BE HAPPY"

Eric Cominski Jr

Chapter 6

Who would have thought Vander built would go on to own the largest shipping yard in America during the Industrial Age? Who would have said with Rockefeller with his family history would go on to pioneer the oil industrial? They were all men of humble beginnings who go an idea and pursued it until the end of time. They were men who made decisions that would go on to change the history of man. They were men who through their dark past and unhelping neighbors would go on to serve the nation. They were men who could work, give and live. They were the men who built America. We would be taught about men like these in our schools and everyday life. Their life would be a symbol of hope and valor for us. But were they like that from the beginning? Rockefeller started working at a very young age and even with that his father – gambler, I presume – still found a way to make life miserable for young Rockefeller. He was always trying to help his mother and instead of going to school, he had to get work. He knew from a very young age he had to do all it takes to succeed. He would eventually go on in life to be the beginning of energy for the nation. The road has never been smooth, anyone who had thread it would tell of its tale. I have mine to tell and so would tens of thousands. But the fortitude is not in how we tell the tale, it is how the tale tells itself. Or do you need to ask yourself who Rockefeller is? I wanted so much to be like that, I want to leave a legacy that would reign in ages. With all my greatness I desire, I had to start somewhere. I had to start my business, I had to make it big.

The road to beginning my clothing line had begun from the battle rap event. But who could tell how the road would be? There is no recipe for success. I have been told and I have forehand experience. You can never know if you would fail or succeed until you start, so I began. The whistle to begin the race has started, to begin my business in earnest with all the legalities and formalities, the ferry is on the water already, the rudder needs a master. Who could tell? If we could tell how the business would go we would put our all in it, but the certainty is a blessing to man rather than the curse we may seem it to be like. It is true if we know our outcomes we might make better choices. But then life would be a jolly ride, which would eventually lead to boredom. Diversity and uncertainty are things that gives life its beauty, our ability to not be able to foretell is our ability to bring out the best.

It is our abilities to forge out different and diverse results even though we had the same tools. Uncertainty is one of the creations of beauty. But uncertainty to me then was not a blessing. It was in later years that I could behold the beauty it begot. Then, I thought beginning a clothing line would be not too hard and not too easy somewhere in between; how hard could that be, right? But, man, it was hard. I couldn't quite put my hand on it. It was different from the textbook definition of starting a business. It was different from the ideal situation that was presented in the business book. It was a world full of probabilities. To the man without the mind, he could – if not careful – lose himself as he would have presumed the ideal to be the real, and the real would seem insane to him. If you ever want to go into business, be so sure you actually want to. No one and I mean no one will know what would happen in the next minute. Your business may fold up, you may run into debt, you may experience so much gain…and luckily you can't be prepared for all situations. Though I have seen people tell me that they are prepared for all uncertainties that might come their way. But words come as easy as we think, an action that speaks when the storm is at bay would tell us how much we are prepared for. Back then, when I was about to go live, I had read extensively I would have devoured the latent of business information. I felt I had everything it took to start, but I wasn't sure what that meant. I mean I felt like Oh! I've got what it takes to take this business to the next level, but if you ask me then that what was it that I have, I just would have replied I have a clothing line that I think is nice. I had a business from the idea that it was nice, but would everyone think it is nice? I couldn't say. But I was dying for acceptance. I would later learn the principle of acceptability in business after so many mistakes. The acceptability of a business. For a business to begin, there are two things involved; the idea and the people behind it. Our balance of both would go a far way to determine our acceptance into the society. And before any business would kick off, those behind the idea should esteem the idea in whichever way they want it to be esteemed. To me, ideas are magical thinking that are real as the chair you are sitting on. They are the ones that arise you mind to conviction. They are the ones that rule your world – "Ideas rule the world", right? But I have come to learn. One could have the greatest idea, and still go on to have a failed business. Ideas are not whole, the other part of it is the execution – the people behind the idea. For a business to succeed, there is a need for a strong connection between those ideas and those who are executing it. Lessons I learnt in later years. But a lot of people I have met are still ignorant of this basic principle to getting started.

I still believe there is a lot of friction between the idea and the people. People would come around and ask, "which one is the better, idea or people?", when they would ask this question, I would smile and recognize with their juvenility. Then I would reply by saying, "For a person that is about to start a business who is thinking that ideas matter than the people behind it; he or she is lazy. And for someone that thinks the people behind it matters more than the idea; then he or she is headed for demise". I would further tell them more about this, "Have an idea and execute it, then you rule the world; don't and you are subject to the world of those who have". I wasn't sound with this sort of knowledge when I started, but I was certain, I had enough to go forward. As a young man, I had faced many hurdles. My tough life has started from when I was a boy to the time I had fans that hate me, to the time I was duped, down to when I was voided….and all through those times, I had learned. I would emphatically say that I didn't know I was learning. It was when I was faced with a similar situation that I would realize how much I know. Thus, the innate of man possesses knowledge the world around him has taught him, if only he would use it in times of need. Our innate hunger for knowledge is never satisfied and can never be. But our innate capabilities of knowledge are without bounds. I would tell people I meet that they have all that they need to succeed within them. You have been created for it. You have got all it takes to get to the peak if only you would look inside. I believe many of us don't look within because of the pressure without. It happens like that many of the times. But our strength in these days is found in our ability to stand back and look further without losing focus that which we need to survive. A famous beverage in my locale this mantra, "Peak, it's within you" – I can't say if they had changed it, but you get it right? I was already struggling. From the business idea and concept to the inception of the business, I had to do it on my own. And when I started like that I knew I was going to have such a wonderful experience – without saying the opposite – to my goal. And with all that went on at that time, I wouldn't flick, I was certain I was ready to make the business big. There was just this conviction that no matter what, I would be great. To this day, it is this zeal that makes me more on higher. Zeal in business, such a great additive if one could have it. Oh! Did I say additive no I meant a compulsion? If you would have anything in business, it must be the zeal. And don't let me start on that because I would tell you of the zeal that drove Steve Jobs out of Apple and back into Apple, I would tell you of the zeal that made

Benz what it is today, I would tell you of the zeal that brought Winston Churchill to become the prime minister of Britain, and I would go on and on about they would have worked with so much zeal their fire could not be extinguished. Some would call it passion. Whatever you call it. You must have it. Yes, I was aware that there would definitely be some hold-offs along the way, but I was also ready – I had been hustling from early life. With my history of hustling and people I had at one time or the other dealt with, I was prepared. Business is like a war. Everyone is out for blood employing every tactic possible. Some might even go on to break the rules – if there are any – some might play by the rules. And it doesn't say with clarity which side would win or lose until the end of the war. You can never say until the last minute what would be at the end of the road, all you have just to do is fight your way till the end. With all this saddle of knowledge, I then venture into the world of business. It was not until I began my clothing line did I realize; one can be so prepared you may never be prepared. I soon would realize that there was no sure way to getting all things right. I was going to learn, and it would take time. I began to take my first steps – baby steps I call it. And I would look into the future and the importance of these steps would tell of the wondrous things to come. I would later realize that the first step I take matters a lot. I would learn that no matter how big the mountain is, your first step if taken right direction would lead you to the top. I would draw emphasis on the first steps in the right direction. Have you ever wondered why many business successes from the start and others – even with the same product do not? Their first steps in the right direction. I have seen two companies grow but one grew into debt and the other from the first day of business advanced into gain. Then I realize how much we would fault if we take our first steps in the wrong direction. And so, I began my designs and getting myself some samples to showcase my clothing line. I had to come up with unique designs as I was not the only one having a clothing line. I was going to put in my best, but I was not that great with designs – what the guy saw the other day was what I would call the slip of hand. Designing was not a big part of what I did. So, I had to find someone who did. When I started the business, I was sure of my strengths and wouldn't deceive myself into believing that one could fit all. NO. I was clear. So, for the designs, I meant this guy called Ant. He was the one responsible for my designs. He did the designs needed for the promotion of the product. Though Ant was a graceful designer and did most of my other logos, the logo for the clothing line was done for me by another guy I met online. I took my time in finding the perfect fit to resonance the name Battle King and it was a success. I had taken my first step. I split the jobs between Ant and the other guy I met online because I was a stickler for effectiveness.

And to be effective – I have learnt – with large jobs, splitting into bits would go a long way to give you the best results. If you ever want to start a business, and you cannot learn to divide and conquer an algorithm I learnt during my days in computing. You may not be able to get the best out of your employees. It was going smoothly with both of them. After I got enough samples, a befitting logo and designs to my product, I headed for the biggest stage I had being; the battle rap events. It was rather a subtle choice than a familiarity option, I had a product, wanted to sell and I need a very big audience. But I could also say I chose to use the battle rap events because of my familiarity with the system, I was once a battle rapper and still had influence – at least that was what I thought. Was the outcome great? I would not describe it as great, but it was receptive which is quite appealing for a start. I also did get feedback on almost all my product, which was good for the product, most were from the hats. I really appreciate these guys as they were the one who seems to be trying to support me. It is very certain, no matter how great your product is, some would love it while some would see how bad you had made the design. At times, to get enough attention for my product I had to give it out for free to the battlers and the performers. I knew I had to do this to get my product noticed, and it was true to start from my locality. The product started on a fine note but was not good enough. Starting a business, I knew would be demanding. The extent I did not know until then. After putting my clothing line out, I had to begin worrying about ways to promote the line. Publication comes after entrance. I had entered, I am now at the point to get noticed by the world around me. To every businessman around. It was just a matter of looking for what would promote what you are doing. I began to ask myself which way to go. What are the ways to promote a product in this age? The answer was the internet or what else? I believe there are lots of ways but the best way to promote your product is the internet and using the social media. At that time, there was no explosion yet like we do now. I was going to use all type of social media platforms. The impact of internet on our daily life cannot go unnoticed as every day we interact with the internet through one way or the other. We have become locked in this new world of ours. Any business that wishes to grow must tap into this source to give its water to the whole world. The internet has made the world a small global village and has provided us with the whole world as the audience. And social media was the best tool to help me promote my product. Have you seen how much people use the social media daily? Or have you not checked your social media account today? Setting up the social media platform for my product was crucial to promoting it.

 I set it up in a jiffy as it did not take the bulk of my time to get it up and running. I didn't need to spend much time on it and I didn't have to. Everything had been made to be easier. If only we would just walk in the way. I had made a few steps into growing my business. I knew the journey was still long, I would be going by taking little steps that matter in the right direction. I was growing my clothing line, and it was getting better by the day. I would say I enjoyed the attention and the presence I had grown for myself I had forgotten about the bigger picture.

I soon realized I have been so focused on the obvious that the bigger picture eluded me. I had been so pinpointed on getting my product to the world, letting the world know about my product that I have forgotten about my brand. My plan from the start was to have a brand, even though the idea was that of a product. But I had sunk in this work of wellness I have forgotten the road that took me here. I was fulfilling the smaller dreams I have forgotten the bigger ones – not that some dreams are small, and some are big. I was living a life that is at the moment, I was forgetting the one I wanted to live, I wanted to be a great brand, everyone would want to be known with, but I have faulted. I would just thank my stars that I realized before it was too late – though I believe it is never too late, but not all the time. So, my dream was a Brand, and I had a product. To some, it would seem like a good achievement, but that was not my dream. But why choose Brand over the product. Brand or Product? During the years of my research in business, I have found out that most companies actually make their brands known rather than their products. When people accept your brand, they would accept your product. You buy an Apple product not because you can understand everything they mean or can use all the functions they have inbuilt, it is because you can understand Apple. You have understood that if it were made by Apple it would be the best of every other. Even with all this knowledge lying around. People still go about daily building a product. I am not saying it is bad. I am just trying to let you know that, products never last, the brand does. Look around in this global world we live in. Bring out a company that focuses on the product and I would bring out one that builds its brand, and then we would compare. And with all these, do not forget there is no brand if there is no product. Therefore, the building should be from brand to products. Not product, product, product… When I knew what I had done. I had to refocus my energy. It was dawn on me that I needed to bring awareness to my brand. The question that follows was how was I to do it? There are no tailored-suit materials or knowledge out there that can tell me what to do and not do in this case.

And with all promotion I have heard and read of, there is the need for a significant amount of money, but all my money has been put into getting the product. What would I do? This would be the first real miss I made. Spending my all on getting the product. I wouldn't say it was a bad decision, but now I would not make the same decision again. I would rather split my spending, though I would spend more on getting the product, I would leave little for building the brand and getting it out to the world. So, it would become a cycle for me. I would get enough to get going, gain from it, and then pump it into the business again. But I had done the deed. I had spent it all on getting the product to the market. And then I knew I had reached a point which would determine my momentum. There was a need to spend more to get more awareness and promote the brand, and there was no money. Such a bad timing. Why would things begin to happen at the bad time? Why would one not have money when he needed it the most? Why would a person's car not start on the day he needed it the most? Is it Karma? Can we ever be sure what it is? Anyways, I figured I had to go back to my roots. I had to begin from where I started. I had to go back to my family and friends. Family and Friends, can one do without all these? Or is it the bond that always brings you back to the family? At the end of the day, they are always who we run to. And we may never be sure they would come through for us. We may never know what they would think of us. But we would try. We would go on to ask them the weirdest help, we would go on to ask for the most inconvenient assistance. We would believe that they would come through for us, and at other times they couldn't because they can't, or wouldn't we may never know. But we would still go. If they wouldn't come through for us now, it means, we wouldn't go back again to them at another time. I found out it can be perplexing and unexplainable the need to fall back to the family.

Though I had my ups and downs with my family, I believe that family is one of the greatest things a man can have. I went back to my friends and family to let them know what I was going through, what I needed to do and how they could help me. But I got the same reply I got when I wanted to start the business, "you have a good thing going on" and "you are doing great" was their responses. But no one wanted to invest in me or be a part of my brand. It was not a shock to me as they had proved it to me the first time, but I do not take it against them. It just taught me to stand for myself that family and friends at times might fail you. So, I was left to help myself. I had to grind my way. So, I looked at other options to further promote my brand. I got some people to wear my clothing and post pictures of them in it online and for these, I had to give it to them for free.

I will have to pay to get my brand promoted; "Giving away free product" was always popping in my head to help promote my product, so I had to buy products just to give away all as a means to promote my brand. Not that that might be a strange technique to go on in business, but it did work. I still wouldn't preach it out to anyone who doesn't have the mind to lose all to do it. But it can be effective as such. And with all my giving out, the technique was moving at a slow pace in promoting the brand, I needed influencers to help promote the brand and I need to pay them. Money has come in again. Money! Money!! Money!!! They would tell you, you need money to make money. What a sad but true statement. Or wouldn't you agree with me? How do you need to make something using that thing? If you want to make your papers you have to use your brains, you wouldn't have to use papers again. But with money the story was different. Business, Money, those two are inseparable. One cannot have a prosperous business without the money. And one should not have a prosperous business that doesn't bring money, it should be unheard. Though I could sit back and complain there is no money, however that would be at the detriment of my business and I did not want to do that, so I had to do something. I saved money, worked overtime and sold old items of mine. By the end of this endeavor, I had made enough sales and my money grew a little, so I plunged it into the brand and marketing it. Day after day, it became challenging to have a clothing line. I was sure I would overcome so I pressed on. All through the way, I sang in my heart that I still believe I shall overcome someday. I was sure that after a while all these struggles of mine would become a story. I have found out that most people spend the money made from the profit on their business, but I realized it should not be so. The profit from the business should be put into the business, and that was what I did. I took the profit to make more profit, yes, not as quite refreshing as spending it, but in the long run, it was the best choice for the business. I kept putting money back into the clothing line for as long as I can remember, and after a while, I have enough in my inventory, it was the point I wanted. I had enough products that I could sell and promote without any unnecessary stretching of my earnings. I was doing fine, and the business was also doing fine, and all the same, I wanted more. It is not uncommon to find humans comfortable with the present. Sometimes we are okay with staying in the familiar although it is mediocre to our dream, we prefer to dwell at the base of the mountain even though the plan was to get to the top. We trick ourselves into believing we have the best life at the base of the mountain we are. Obscurity is fallen on us and we cannot see beyond what we have.

But I was not like that, I knew my plans. – to get to the top – so no obscurity would dare befall me. I was clear as the day everyday as I work. I knew I wanted more than I was having. And at this present moment, what I wanted more was to move beyond the locale. I wanted to be known in the whole state of Virginia. I was not satisfied with being the glory in my locale. I wanted to go, as they now say, viral. I wanted to be known. I had begun my clothing line in Portsmouth, and I was known in Portsmouth, but it is just a city, I wanted to be known throughout the state. I told myself if I would achieve this feature. I need to have a team. To achieve such as space, I need many arms to go around. Many legs to work with, and many heads to think with. I needed a team, and a good one in fact. Teams, I needed one. Teams are very essential to the success of a business as putting all the work on yourself is a pathway to the demise of the business. I knew I had to get a team that would represent the best of the business, but I was not a people's person – a displacing weakness of mine. Gathering a team would be a very hard thing to do and I was going to be bad at it. Do not get me wrong, I get along with people, networking, yes, but on the personal level, no. But I had to do this for the sake of my business and from then I was on the lookout for who is the best fit. Finding a team is not only about asking questions to be sure of who that person is or not and lots, it is more than that as every member of the team are now bounded by the goal of the company or business. Every member should be part and feel the part of the team, it was more than getting people for positions within the business, and rather it was how well they would handle the business and one another. I figured that there is no readymade team, you cannot say for sure they would accept each other, but if everyone on the team can accommodate the other, they can turn out to be a good team. And if a good team executes a dollar-idea it might turn to a million-dollar product, but if a bad team executes a million-dollar idea it is certain to result in a disastrous product. I knew I had to be careful. In the process of finding a team, I got thinking of how to transit to another level, I just did not know how. I had done almost everything you could do as a clothing line, you mention it. As I thought, I soon realized that I had been thinking about the brand, the clothing line all the way. As a matter of fact, there were about twenty brands of clothing line in Virginia started by people, and it evidently became a lot that I was thinking to try something else. I did not like to put myself in a box, I had struggled from start to have a free and exciting life.

During my thought train, as I dived into the world of silent words that comes from the heart I discovered I wanted to begin another business. And what business would that be? I wanted to do something that would give my clothing brand awareness. What would be the perfect answer? What! What!! What!!!

"DON'T BOX YOUR SELF IN, DO MORE AND DO DIFFERENT THINGS"

Eric Cominski Jr

Chapter 7

Then it came to me, Magazine! Then I recall the story of one of America's finest, Elon. Elon, the very one of SpaceX, Tesla…when wanted to start something in the aerospace sphere. So, he travelled to China to meet a bunch of aerospace suppliers to get some necessary things for his launch vehicle, who didn't take him seriously the first time. But he wouldn't stop. He travelled again, and this time, he was able to meet them. But in course of the meeting, he stormed out believing the price was too much. The price of building a rocket to him was more than the price of launching one. How could that be? To him, the idea seems preposterous. And that was when he knew he wanted to go into the aerospace business. He wanted to start building rocket that even a common man can get the necessary items and start building his own. He wanted to build a rocket where no one would see how unreasonable it is to build a rocket that was exorbitantly high. He wanted to do something, and he knew it was an aerospace company. And that was the birth of SpaceX. Earlier, Elon has just left the company he created with his brother and the advances from it was what made him think of going into a new business, and not only that he also fell in love with the outer space right from childhood which is evident in his love for Isaac Aminov, Foundation Series. Then I concur that our drive to have more would give us more in itself. Think to get better and you would be better. The will has its power, and our ability to think we would surmount and get into another business makes us want to go into another business. I would quite agree that not everyone could start a new business after another. But we should all grow. We should all leave our comfort zone. "Life begins at the edge of your comfort zone", a saying I feared might be too true we would never realize if we don't step out of our comfort zone. I was going to start leaving out of my comfort zone. I was going to get into the Magazine business. What! Yes, Magazine was the next stop for me in the line of my business. It seemed great – at that time at least – and would definitely bring awareness to my clothing line. But not only did I not know anything about it, I could quite say for sure where to start. The team that I so much needed, I couldn't get, I was left to begin the race myself, whether anyone would join in I can never say. After the idea [starting a magazine business] leapt into me and I was certain I was going on to do it.

    I looked look back and I felt satisfaction run through my veins that I got the idea at last. I will forever have a zeal for more, but when I got this idea it moved me up a pace and at this point, I felt very satisfied. I was satisfied but I would later find out that I was not content, I was panting for more as the deer pants for water. To me, this moment, anytime I got an idea, I would always appreciate the work of creation. It has all been within us, all this time. We just need to press the right combination to release it to the world. And that was what I would do. I would be pressing the right combination of energy into it. But then I had to take a break. There are moments in life when some certain decisions we make really make the world for us. Though these decisions might not be the breakthrough kinds, but when you figure out something or you were able to make a certain choice which would advance you, you should ensure you enjoy the moment. Celebrate your small victories and be committed to getting bigger ones. Victories always have a way of pushing you to do wonders. Man's ability to enjoy and live in them is an evidence of not his own ways but the way of creation and the appreciation thereof. I began my research on producing a magazine and I found out I had some of the things needed not many. I wanted to start badly as I felt I was ready. I just stepped on the gas and on to the highway. To produce a magazine, the things you essentially need are; a designer, a writer and an editor, a team. I needed a team and so I went out looking for one. It was already hard to find a team for my clothing line – I couldn't quite find one, now I need a team for my magazine. Thus, I discovered the importance of teams. Team, Together Everyone Attains Much, as one of my Lecturers used to put it. Is embedded in the fabric of success. We couldn't do it all by ourselves. But I looked back to myself then and realized it was not so, for me. I began looking for a team. Looking for the best pairs of eyes that would see the problem as a problem and probably even more. People who would push themselves to the extremes that impossibilities become possibilities. I was looking and searching while hoping and praying. I couldn't have agreed more, it was such an interesting search as I encountered diverse personalities. I talked to people, saw what they were doing what and how they could fit into what I wanted. I searched for people who were like-minded who have the same drive as I perhaps even more. It was not so simple to find people who can be what you envisioned or what you want. I searched far and near, did my best to find the best fit for the team but I was always short. Who faulted? I couldn't quite get it; why I wasn't finding people. Have you ever tried to look for people with the same drive as you? Then you might realize you might be the same one with that drive.

And you would wonder is it because you are unique? And you would pray that you may not be, so you could find people. But you shouldn't, things would not be the same forever. If there is anything that is constant, it is change. If you do not have someone to go on with then go on yourself. I am sure, and I believe that help will come along the way. Just begin. I began to ask questions. I was getting more confused. Was I not good at searching? Or are there people without the same zeal as I? I could not tell for sure. I just kept mute to the game the world was playing. I had played my own cards, and life itself is withdrawing hoping to see I would flicker. But I wasn't, and I am not going to start then. Thus, I continued searching… All the while I had been working with DOT R – He is one of my investments. He already had some equipment, but I gave him all my studio I had to add to his and give him a better setup. With the help of DOT R, I had made some connections with artists and producers and because of this, I could get much content for the magazine. Content to any magazine was crucial, though the design plays an inviting role, the content plays an engaging role to its readers. If I wanted to catch the audience attention, I had to have a great design and I would need a better than ordinary content to keep the readers stick to it while watching out for the next. Getting the first issue of my magazine out was going to be a painstaking process I was certain of it. And this first issue would also be the one that would put the brand out and it needs to be a bold introduction for the brand. I need to be great at first and greater with the rest. I wanted to put local artist businesses etc in the magazine. Doing that would bring great importance to the magazine. As a business every time you come up with an entry product you want it to be a great feat so that your customers would look forward to the next ones. I did not want to rush it as I wanted to make an indelible impact in getting the magazine out, so everyone could see what was next for me. And with the search for the team, I was getting nowhere. It felt like the universe was against me. I didn't have expertise in this line of work. I just believe that it would work out. Believing was what kept me true all through my days. I would call it the days of believing. The days when it seemed like I was going the wrong way and felt I was going the right way. I wouldn't be able to explain my choices to everyone around as they told me, "You have a thriving clothing line already, Why Magazine?" I would not be able to answer that question until later years. For the magazine, I wanted to keep it at the entertainment platform. Sticking to something out of everything was what I should do. I should have a niche. I believe there are times you need to have a niche and focus on it. This time was that time. I should have a niche and make it mine.

I was already familiar with the entertainment platform as such it would be an easy drive in for me. I was going to interview rap artists and producers. I didn't realize how much I would be shocked. Till this present moment, I couldn't quite understand somethings. It can be so frustrating that you want an answer, but that answer would never be coming. One of the things that baffled me then and still is now is the fact that some of the interviewees did not show up. It would not have baffled me if we're asking them to pay. But I wasn't. I think they say people like free things – not as a sign of disrespect, but have you seen free days at the mall. Why wouldn't they just show up? I was doing the thing and it would be out to the world. It was a chance to get themselves out there without heavy strings attached. I may never be able to tell why they wouldn't show up. Now one could say maybe I was bad. And that could be right. But I have seen people recognize themselves with villain voluntarily and I wasn't one yet. And the worst thing I had ever do till then would be better than an of those that people readily associate themselves with. So, to my mercy, I was not guilty of being a bad influence. Most of the people I set the interviews up with did not show up and when I asked them to do the interview they seemed like they did not want to do it. "What's up with these people?" I would ask myself. No objections I was just starting, but I was going to go places why won't they at least take that chance on me? And who the heck does not want to be in a magazine? I would just head on and see what I could do without them. I would later learn an essential lesson in later years; just because you think you need something doesn't necessarily mean you not having it would result in failure. I move on with the rest of the aspect of the magazine. I wanted to put a model section in the magazine; basically, a model who wanted to get some exposure. I would put their best shots in the magazine and their contact information, so people can see their work and contact them if they needed to work with them. Modeling was never easy so putting them in the magazine was my way of helping them to help me –if you know what I mean. I did my best, but it was hard getting models. I could not quite figure out why I had trouble in almost all the aspect of the magazine; getting to interview artists and producers who did not turn up was something, finding models was another. It was really hard for me. But I was not going to stop now, I had begun the journey, I will not stop until I reach the finish line. I still couldn't find a model. At this point, I looked at myself if nothing was wrong with me. But there was nothing wrong with me. I was in something called the business world and I was interacting with people of instantaneous gain. No one would wait for me to get known. They all want to be known right then. This I would learn in my later years. I went on to creating a channel on YouTube to do videos for people to see. It was another form of content for the magazine. I was bent on making the magazine a big break, and I would do all I can to get a fantastic content for it. Although it was hard getting people to be in the magazine, it would not stop me as I pressed forward; I was going to grow with or without them. At the end of my lookouts for people to be in the magazine; I found some people who would do an interview and wanted to be in the magazine, Thus, there could be a silver lining in the midst of the troubled cloud. But I was still short of the things I needed to declare the first issue of the magazine done. So, I stepped back into my family. My family and yours is one that I would ever hammer you should keep in contact with. You should take them with you on every step of the way. They would always be there for you. And along the way, I got DOT R. to be in the magazine, at this time he was a well-known producer, and I used my sister for the model section. Also, it was around this time that my uncle finished his mixtape, and I talked to him, so I could use it for the review section. He was cool with it and so I was moving forward not at the speed I anticipated but I was moving towards my goal. Was I content at moving at this manner? I was not but what more could I do. Progress I know was all that matters and progressing well was the goal. And I was doing just that. It was slow I know but I was moving. It is better to be moving like a snail than not to move at all, right? I also wanted to put a cipher in the magazine and on the channel, but it was hard to get everyone that said they would do it to actually do it. It is easier said than done. They were dead in the water. Man, I have experienced a lot of rejection. As I write and recall all these memories, my heart hurts and I felt sorry for my old self. I felt sorry for how he had to go without nothing to assure or have his back. I felt sorry that he had to be in it alone. I was still struggling to climb the hill; the hill was slippery. Rain had fallen the previous night. I had chosen a bad time. Would I then descend and come to climb another day? Never. I was going to climb it no matter what. The magazine was proving to be a success, but I did not have a story worth the cover page. Yeah, the cover page, that first eye catching thing of the magazine which should spill out its story. I did not want to do the cover page myself, so I approached several people I deemed fit to help sell the brand to its best, but all to no avail. And now they would say I am making it about myself. I didn't want my magazine to be about myself that was why I stepped out. But as you see no one came forward. Please don't ever say that I made it about myself. That was my thought when I remember those familiar words, "you made it about yourself".

After a long back and forth, I decided to put myself on the cover page. As I look back, it felt as if all through those time, I was always meeting failure, nobody was coming up to help me, I was left to myself. It was a struggle I had to win. Since I was going to be on the cover page; I needed a story and what would the story be? I realized there was no bigger story than what I am doing; that was my story. I put a quick page section on me and what I was doing. I included a little background of myself and the rest was about me making moves. – hustling. I knew the feedback I would get for putting myself on the cover page, but what could I do? I called out to people to help out, but no one would help. And I do not care about what anyone will have to say after that. Although, I had a lot of let downs about people getting involved in the making of the magazine. I am grateful to those who stepped in and let me put them in my first issue. At the end, I was doing everything myself. I would get help with the review as I did not want to do that one myself. I was doing everything not because I wanted it to be so, but because most people that I wanted and talked to, to be a part of the magazine was no show. So, I was left to myself. I also did get help with the logo and some of the designs, but most of the designs I did myself. I had to sit down to do the design on each page while piecing it together. It took the bulk of my time, but I had no option I had been left to myself. It was time that it would take for me to get to where I am going. I was going to put the energy in it. I was going to go all the way to the end. After asking for help all around and there seem to be no one willing to help; I stop asking. Have you been there? When you just get tired? When you just don't want to do it again? That was the point. I was tired. I couldn't tell people anymore that they should be a part. I was tired of people telling me that I got a good thing going on, but they would not put a single drop of energy to help, I was tired. So, I kept true to myself and went on the way. If I was to succeed I would and now with no help from anyone I just had to put in more energy into it. With all my energy, I still felt alone. But I wasn't. I had my family, friends, and people who would eventually believe in me. That thought alone reminded me that I was not alone. For the photo shoots in the magazine, I got help from Mr. C., such a lovely guy. He had previously been responsible for taking most of my family photographs and was the one we used at our wedding. Though he was a busy man, he helped out in his free time. He never said why he chose to help me, but I could tell that it was because he saw a drive in me trying to do something for myself and he wanted to be part of it. He was someone I could count on and his help was priceless. He was part of the few that actually stood by to help with my dream.

You would realize as you move through life that not everyone can be there for you, but the ones that are there would make such a gracious impact in your life. I am always thankful to Mr. C. As one of his help outs, I set up sessions for the magazine and no one showed up. To me, it was already anticipated, but I did not wish they would do it to Mr. C. But he understood that those who did not show up did not have enough zeal to move with me. We arranged these shoots for multiple times, and he was down for it. It was like once or twice that at least one person would show up. But he [Mr. C] understood. What a gracious fellow. With a new business, I just prayed that even though with even bad turns they encounter, they would get to their own Mr. C, I felt it was a cycle that was bent on doom. Every now and then I would talk to people and they would be down with it, then I would arrange the time for the shoot and no one would be around. It was frustrating to be in such scenario. Sometimes, I do wonder what happened as when I met them, they would promise such a wonderful outcome but at the end, it is but a fart in the thunder. I must note that I was also disappointed but not dejected, at times I felt rejected, but I suspected it was because I was going places. People would not always be there for you. Either believe it or you don't things would happen like that. Though you might see someone who is very enthusiastic about your dream, he may never be around to help. You are the only one who would not leave yourself stranded. And if you do. Good luck! Around this time, Ant, the guy that had been helping with my designs, wanted money for the logos he did for me. Why would he come with his own issue at this time? It was bad timing. I told him as soon as I got money I would pay him and at the time I could not pay for the logos he did for me. Truly, I knew he was really helping out, but I was not doing this to hurt him, he really did great for me. I thought he was a part of my team. Him doing logo and designs for me with out asking for money at first made me fell that he was down with my movement. But no one could tell the intent of another man; if we could there would be more understanding. And I think it was the understanding that was not there that made him think I was undermining his impact on the magazine as he went on to post on Facebook about having the rights to his designs and how I decided to give away for free all the clothing I had his design on. To me, this was hurting as I had been thinking of him as a team member, that he was part of the team till I had a breakthrough. I was even thinking of him helping out with the designs of the magazine, but his words have put a bad taste in my mouth. I had nothing against him as I would also want to get paid and I knew why he had to be paid.

I reached out to him about having a sit-down talk with him, we never did but we cleared things out, but things would never be the same again. Watch your six senses I would tell you. Watch what your eyes see, what your skin feels, what your nose smells, what your hand touch, what your ear hears and what your mouth says. Watch it, it can be great for business or otherwise. At this point, I had a model – my sister –. A producer – DOT R –, and an artist – one of those I interviewed. I put some advertisement for people that had their own business in it and I added battle rap events that would be coming up. It was nearing completion, and I was damn happy. It was one of the feelings of accomplishments that I always looked forward to. I would soon be done with the race and face another phase I was not going to call it quits. I had a project for the review section – my uncle's mixtape, my cover story and then my clothing line. As I near completion with the magazine, my sense of accomplishment flourished. I got more excited about the magazine. I couldn't wait to get it out to the world. All my troubles had finally paid off. I had finished my magazine and was going to publish it using Blurb; it is an effortless way to get things published and printed for a magazine.

Apart from getting the content of the magazine ready, I had to deal with the legalities involved; the ISBN number to be precise. I sorted out the ISBN number and Blurb helped with finding things that might affect the print of the issue if the picture were not great enough and all the printings necessities. I did my best by getting the magazine ready for printing, and Blurb made the rest a stress-free ride to publication. On its way to publication, I realized it had turned into a one-person thing and I needed more for the magazine than I had. I knew I needed to look for anything to do other than this magazine because of how hard it was even to get started. I had to hold on. I would just publish it like that in later years. I couldn't quite find the story I was looking for. So, I moved on and away from the magazine corpus, while investigating what more I could do to make me happier. It was true I had concentrated a lot of energies on making the magazine a possibility and I did my best. And I had a product, but I would not want a product that I would not be proud of. If I would do something, I would rather do it well or not do it at all. I want to be able to make reference to it in years to come that I was the pioneer of this. This made me realize that not every idea that comes into your head would hold up to your love, we can have millions of ideas, but the best ones are those that sprung out of love. I had to recall my love. It had to be from love, love is central to beginning great things; I had to do things that I loved. What have I done that I loved?

That would be music, I have always loved music, but I was not looking to get back into music anytime soon. But I told myself I was going to do at least one album before it is all said and done, but now I could not. The next thing I loved was playing video games. I was a game head. Thus, I figured. To the gaming world!' The new voyage has started. I was going to start a video game studio. Many people told me I should take a break. I just couldn't because my dream could not wait. I just dived right in.

"IT'S ALWAYS YOUR FAULT, TAKE BLAME, IT MAKES IT EASIER TO TAKE CREDIT FOR THE WINS"

Eric Cominski Jr

Chapter 8

My journey with the video game started. I have been told, "If you want to start something, start the minute you think of it". It is called the willpower. I have seen people with great ideas, but they wouldn't start something until after a long time. And when they are about to start, someone had beat them to the dream. So, I conclude, the dream you have might not be yours alone. There might be someone elsewhere having that same dream as yours, your ability to bring to life is what distinguishes both of you in success. Every day you wake up from your dream. Remember that someone somewhere might beat you to it. It is those who wake every day and beat towards their dream and bring it to the world that is known and respected. They are the ones the world wants to know; no one wants to know if you have good intention or not, all they want to know is what have you done with the good intention. Within every man is the saddle to success. Few of those that want it and work towards it get it. The United States, during the space race, birthed a dream of sending the first man to the moon. They wouldn't deter and worked for years from the day President Fitzgerald made the proclamation to the day Apollo mission was completed, they wouldn't rest. Even with the rest of the world working towards that same dream, they beat everyone to it and went on to erect the United States flag on the moon. That was the mind that has a dream and beat everyone to it. I was going to be of that mind also. I wanted to so much go into gaming. I have a dream of owning and building my own game. Though I had never done it, I was going to start then, and I was going to start well. But one could say I still had the scent left from my encounter in making my magazine. Yeah, I did. I was just not the kind of guy who would spend a long time on already grown trees. I was focused on making the smaller ones bigger. That was the man I was and the man I am. And not that I wouldn't care for the grown trees anymore, but that its soil would not become a dirt to my garment in the process of toil. I had sown, it had grown. I had sweat, it had produce. There was no going back. So, I shook it off and I was anew. Forgetting things of the past and looking unto the future. I believe that is how you should be to be able to go on to do exploit. You shouldn't let anything deter or defer you from pursuing dreams after dreams day after day. People would complain that you have done enough, let them be.

It is their opinion, what matters most is have you fulfilled your dream? The end of the race should not be when people around you say it is over. The end of the race is when you say it is over. You might be spent, you might not have all it takes. But just move on in the power of your dreams. If you are going to go far, you need to be like that. You need it to be able to move fast and smart. I have seen people starting a new business from another, move so slow you would wonder if they were the ones that actually did start the first business. I would soon realize starting your first business is tough, but another business after a successful one is even riskier. We can all fall victim to knowing. When you start your first business, you do not know anything. Which is actually good for business and might be the best thing. So that you have to learn a lot of things. But when you are about to start another, you would need to unlearn and re-learn something which you would presumably think you already know. And that is the risk I am pointing out. As you start another business, you would soon realize that things have changed – they are meant to. And if you wouldn't shake off the dirt and glory of the past life. You might go on to flutter in distress and run your business to the ground. With the video game, I was going to fight this one without the pains and glory I encountered with the clothing line. I was going to go all out and fight like it was my first and last. I began research on video game production. I investigated making video games and what I would have to do to start my own video game studio. I went through a series of documentation, articles, and discoveries. The basic things that are needed and that I discovered are: To start a video game. You need the story, which can also be called the gameplay. And it has to be an interesting and captivating one with lots of anticipation because you want to keep your users locked in till the end. After you have gotten the story you need the game designers. These are the ones that work with the story to create the characters that depict the one portrayed in the story in the most amusing ways. And from there you are the one who would go on to the game developers, who will work with the Game Engine to produce what you want. Every one of these takes a significant amount of time. If your game is not one that has levels – which probably every interesting game should have – then you are looking to a longer period of time to produce an outstanding game. If by everything, you were able to get a good story. Then you look for the promoters, or investors – people who would fund the production. That is when you can hire game designers, developers and everyone that you need. It was going to take time, money and people. Have you ever seen the credits of a game?

When I saw what I was up against and I realized it was more than a one-man endeavour. Then it became clear to me this was not a one man's job; I need a team. Still shocking right? How much I am sort for a team and at every point, on the journey, I still need a team. It was overwhelming for me, as I have always stood out as a one-man army. Now I was going to need a team; it was too much for me. It was like I should back down, but I caught myself in the act and cub myself. I am going to still search for the very team that I desire and need. I haven't fared well all these whiles with teams. I couldn't say what would happen. But I was determined I was going to find out. I was not going to leave my ball un-played. I still think that I could have said no and do any other thing apart from gaming. But it was so easy to say no and back out of things. And I was not in for the easy part. I wouldn't want to get it if it were easy. If it were easy everyone would have it. It is because it isn't that I want it. Backing out was what everybody does, and I was not everybody, I was different. When never I am in some tough situations like this; when the end seems to know no end. I would have asked myself when thing get tough for the million-dollar company, what would they do? I do this mostly; ask these questions. Whenever I am in these sorts of situations I ask myself what would my dream company do? Would they go the effortless way out? Would they take the easy way out? Would they leave the problem because it was tough? Would they? No, they wouldn't. They would try and try until it worked. They would try and fail and try and fail until they get the result they want. All the while they would learn. This is what leads to invention. Man's ability to fail forward. In business, it is very possible that you would fail. You might fail more than you would ever do or fail lesser than you ever can. But the probability of failing is on the business, and failure is not the problem. It has never been. It is what you do with it that matters and breaks bondage. It is what you do with it that becomes a breakthrough. To me, failure is a way to learn. It is actually an old method most people are unaware of. It had been around for ages. Failure is not about the scores of the company that goes down, it is about what the company would gain from going down. Failure is not about being wrong, it is about knowing what made you wrong and never returning to it again. It is about finding new ways to do something. You fail, you learn from it and try again. The lesson that failure teaches are imbibed in a selected few. So, one has to be careful to be among the selected few because when failure comes. Its [failure] activities are like that of rushing water would clutter your mind, you wouldn't be able to see the light that comes after.

    Beware so that the lesson failure wants to teach might go unlearn and the mind is filled with disastrous opinions after it [failure] had left. And I was going to do just that. I was going to start even though I don't know if I would fail or not. But I was willing to try and fail and learn and continue the cycle until I got what I wanted. I just would be lucky. To be true, video game was a whole new level; an entirely different environment actually. I was looking at doing video game as a hobbyist, but with the stress why not get paid while at it. Getting paid is not always the aim and should not always be but getting paid while enjoying what you do is a good way to spend my life. In this situation, you do not look forward to the end of the day and start of another, but you want each day to last longer. You would not be motivated by the amount of cash that comes in but by a greater motivation; a motivation of love. If you are ever in love with the right things and they are able to source you. You would go on to live a life of love. Take it from someone who had tried it. In the course of my research, I found out there was much to be put into it but it was rather easy to get into the market as far as just doing it is concerned. But to make it big you need a very good game; which would be the result of a good gameplay or concept, and a talented team. I indicated a talented team because only talents rules in this industry; it is not about having a team that can do this and that. Rather it is about having a team that is skilful and creative. In this industry [gaming industry]; head knowledge is subject to talents as talent is the boss. When I continued searching I would soon realize that although game development requires lots of people with the know-how and creativity. It is not impossible to make a game as a single person, it was just going to take a lot of time and time was all I have. I can still remember how happy I was when I stumbled on this revelation – I could do game development as a single person. I wasn't sure I was going to, but I did. Being a one-man army was my greatest move and I loved it, and this news was by far the one I always wanted. With this great news, my blood started pumping with the enthusiasm and no worries about getting a team. What a news could do to you! One lesson I learnt at this point was this; search further don't stop. When I started reading about building a video game, most resources I found were talking about getting a team together. I could have just stopped there. But I wanted to work in my comfort zone. So, I searched further for what I wanted, and my joys knew no bound. Every time we want to start a new thing. We have something in mind but along the way, we may find out that it might not be possible. But if we would go on and continue searching, we might find just that thing we have been looking for all this time. I can build a video game on my own. What! I was going to start building my video game on my own. It was what I wanted to do and doing it on my own adds so many flavors to it. I commenced with everything I have got. I got started with the logo for the video game. Logos are the first thing the market would see, and I need to make it as inviting and unique as possible. I was already tired of fighting people to be part of my team, but I needed help anyway. I couldn't still do everything on my own. I was not everything and can never be, I can only try and if I could, my strength would be zapped before my time is up. I knew I had to find help, just after that then I was going to take a different route. I was going to use the internet. So, I went online, and I found a company to do designs and logos around the clock for $5 a logo. It was a good deal. What I did was to get the logo design initiated and fix things I wanted with it. And I knew my way around the computer to effect the changes that I wanted with the designs and the logos. I had gone online, and the experience was smooth. As I progressed, I realized if I could not get someone to do something, I was going to learn it. That is the spirit; if you cannot get people to help out with something, then you go out of your way to learn it, and at the end, it is a win for you. Therefore, nothing was going to stop me from getting to the top of my goal; neither nonchalant attitude I got from people nor the absence of a knowledge was going to stop me. The first game I wanted to do was RPG game, Role Playing Game – the kind of game where the game player is playing the role of a fictitious character and building an RPG game is hard. RPG is one of the difficult games there is to make. I knew it was difficult, but I wanted to do this badly. I have heard that if you were about to start something new you should start small; if that worked for them fine, but for me, I was going to start mounting from the highest peak, I was going to learn the hard way up. This might be uncommon, but I can say this way works. Not everyone is built to start from small things and not everyone has the courage to go the hard way. With no discrimination from my part, I just think that we are all configured in different ways. Knowing what constitutes us would be our gain in the long run. We would never be the same. No two things in this world would ever be the same. Research is the backbone for a confidential adventure. If you are sure you want to do something, you have got to read about everything and anything you can find on it, you have to put all in – either all in or all out. That was my code. I devoted bulk of my time to learning about things that matter to the business and I was pretty much successful. I motivated, myself to do everything and I always had to remind myself every time things were going awry that I was going places.

I went on to learn about making RPG and in the course of my research I found out about RPG Maker MV. It was user-friendly and the scripting was good – the scripting language was Ruby. I was satisfied that I had all I need to move on. And research pays. The RPG Maker MV is an interface that helps one make RPG and it makes it so easy I could not quite believe it. If you could give your all to something, you would eventually get the result you wanted and would be pleased you started it the first place. I learned to use the program in a jiffy and thereafter paid someone to write the story for me. I also got a person to design the characters for me. This was thrilling for me; making video games was unheard of when I was a kid but now I could. I was so excited. Though the road had been rough, I had been able to scale through with joy at the end of the tunnel. As I waited on the story for the video game and the characters; as I had outsourced it, I continued work on the magazine and did it more. I also put the video game in the magazine as an exclusive. I picked a name to match what I was doing with my clothing brand. I was going to call the magazine "Throne Magazine". The name of the video game studio went on to be "Royalty Unleashed". Everything was going well at this point and all my endeavors had been progressing at a reasonable rate. But when I thought about all of what I was doing, it was going in the direction of the CEO-like thing I never wanted. Not that I did not want to be a CEO, I want to be, but better than that, I want to own a chain of business. I did not want to be CEO on a business rather I want to be CEO of CEOs. That has been the plan, I was not going to back down now. Thus, started looking at my brand value. It finally occurred to me to build my brand; I had to begin incorporating everything together and begin creating my legacy. I had always wanted that. Legacy was what I would have left when I am going out of this world. Brand is what would tell people about me. I need a very good Brand to ensure a lasting legacy, and a lasting legacy would be an evidence of a great brand. They both have to work together. It is true there was no legacy left for me, not that I detest not having been left a legacy, I wanted more for my family. I wanted to leave a legacy for them that would speak through generations. I was going to bring everything I have been doing: the clothing line, the magazine, and the video game under one umbrella. I was going to make it all come under one voice. I started looking and the best fit. I need to take my time to get the best fit for everything I had been doing from the beginning till then. I needed to go smart. I knew it was going to take time, so I did take time for myself. I took a break to think of the best I could come up with.

"THERE IS ALWAYS SOMEONE THAT WANTS IT MORE THEN YOU SO WORK HARD"

Eric Cominski Jr

Chapter 9

I had to bring everything I was doing under one banner. I had to create a name, they would all bear. I finally came up with the name BATTLE KING INC, it was going to be the head of my struggles. I was doing a clothing line; a magazine and I have a video game studio and they are all to go under this incorporation. I was doing something with myself. I was myself. I was nearing myself. I was getting to that point. When I got the name from the brand I looked back and realized how far I had come. And as far as money and time was concerned, I had been by myself from the start. I did not detest not having help but helped never showed up. It didn't mar me, it would go on to make me. This was me from the start, I would be proud of that. Why do almost every entrepreneur have an issue with their family? Have you ever wondered why? Who has the greatest rate of divorce? Celebrities, right? I couldn't quite understand their situation until I got into that situation. I would learn after much criticism from my side that I could also be leaning towards the edge. I could also be going the way I never want to go. I could only thank my wife at this point, she was my rock. Around this time [when I brought everything I was doing together] my son was already growing up. I didn't want to repeat the scene that happened with my dad with him, but I couldn't help it. And I could never know I was on that path until I was cautioned. When we are on our journey to greatness, our focus on the end may make us elude the presence of the present. We may be so focused on the future we want for ourselves that we forget the present we live in. I had been so focused on the present, I had forgotten about the most important thing to me – my family. As I remember this time, I feel sorry and bad that I had not been there for them. I could complain, but it was my choice to choose to spend lesser time with them. My wife came to me and told me how worried she was about how little the time I spent with the family. I had no excuse; I was guilty of the charge. My wife, Casheem, had been a superwoman from the beginning and had held up the house while I was busy working around. I knew I had to find time for my family and I knew quite well that it was going to be hard. It was already hard managing the clothing line, magazine and the video game studio. I just knew then that I needed to find time for myself. These are some realizations that came to me at this point. It was crucial beyond reasonable doubt that I had been so busy and involved I have forgotten about some of the things that matter – myself and my family.

And it was not that I wanted it to be like that, it was just how I had been moving things to help me get to my dream. One of the main reasons I started my company besides the fact that I love to hustle and make money is my family. I wanted to leave something for my son to have so he can have something from his father. I have been so focused on the end, I had forgotten the present. Though they are true when they say, "The end justifies the means", but when does the end justify the means when the means that makes the end a meaning is lost? I had to refocus and make more time for my family. There were quite a number of things running through my mind, but I have to move things around in a jiffy to get things to where I wanted them, so I could spend more time with my family. Finally, I decided to slow down a little on the company and spend more time with my family. I realized I had to wait for the moment to get this done in the way I wanted. The wait would later be a blessing rather than a mere wait. It was at this point that I had time to reflect on what I was doing. I realized that I could be so caught up in what I was doing, I would forget to reminisce on things – thing before now and things after. Yeah, I could be doing fine, but we are thinking man. Thinking has been what makes us different from the rest of the perk. We are the thinking man. And for us the issue might be that we do not think, it is with the depth of our thinking. Most of the time our thinking is thinking fast, who would be the first person to get to the moon, who would be the first to build an autonomous vehicle… which is good. It is what actually brings development to man. But how much time do we spend on deep thinking? There is the ability innate in us to do great things if we could think both ways. Thinking wide which would determine our breadth and thinking deep which would determine our depth. And if we get to the point we refuse to use the thinking power of man and let our actions be determined by our energy we would soon exhaust ourselves. That is why it is necessary to ask ourselves and remind ourselves at every point in time that what we are doing and why we are doing it. During my time of reflection, I started looking at Eric Thomas videos. Eric Thomas is a powerful speaker one thing that he does that grabbed my attention was how he keeps it real. It is one thing to motivate someone, it is another to motivate someone and keep it real. At one time, one of my friends was talking about how some of the motivational speeches instead of motivating make you feel lesser than them – a reason he dislikes them. But Eric Thomas was different, he had what I wanted and did his job – motivated me. He motivated me to focus more and do what I need to do to be where I want to be. Then was where I set a low but high goal to have a million-dollar company.

I kept that in my head, I studied it and I researched about million-dollar companies and looked at what I needed to do to get there. I realized having a goal is what most people do, but achieving it is what elect few do and that's what makes them different. I was on my way to be different. I had to study and learn from those who had walked this path. One of the greatest mistakes I believe we make is we want to create an entire new recipe for success for ourselves while there are many out there that we can just tweak a little to match our taste. Sometimes our thirst for success is far beyond our capacity to reach for it, which is quite good, but we must be willing to bridge that gap by learning, which most of many times we do not want to do. Our innate desires success but if we do not move forward with zeal we are at fault. It was clear that I had invested too much time and money to back out. I had to take a break and find myself. I would go on to have clean thinking which would refine my way of life and go on to change things for the better. People who have seen what I did and envisioned what I need to do to get there do ask me if I ever think about quitting. The answer is yes! I think about quitting all the time, but I would not quit at any time. I am certain I can surmount the greatest mountains if I can just persevere. And quitting is the easy way out, I do not want the easy way out, and as they say, "quitters never win, winners never quit" or is it the other way around? I cannot say. But the point is you cannot quit and expect your dreams to come true, you have to come through for your dreams to come true. Quitting is never an option for me. I would lose more if I quit than I would if I moved on. My time, money and family has been focused on this so why would I quit? I had gotten to a point that quitting would be expensive for me. I would advise anyone that comes to me for help with these: Put in so much work into the vision you have to the extent that quitting would cost you so much if you dare quit. If you do so, then you would have sealed your faith towards failing and you would just go on to do exploits. I was so focused and given my all that quitting would have to be bigger than quitting for me to quit. After the break, I was back at work, but this time with a clearer perspective. I had washed my face with the waters of memories and looked at the mirror for reflection, I was truer to myself even more. I continue working on modern designs for clothing, getting ready to finish the magazine and publish the first issue. The break was getting the better out of me. I would go on to see the impact of rest in all the aspect of my business. Rest they say is sweet after the day's work. But our abilities to find rest is the problem. We become so occupied in all we are doing we wouldn't want to stop.

It is true, you might not feel like you need any, things might even be going so well rest would be a bad break for you. With all those truths. The Truth is still embedded that, rest calms the soul. It gives the body space to go wild. It gives the mind the space to come to a place and put his head to the ground. It gives way to thinking without boundaries. But never rest for longer than you can afford. If you are of the opinion that you cannot afford to rest, that would be bad. And if too much rest would cost you more than anticipated, cut it. I had rested and was going back into hustling. With the magazine and clothing going smoothly. I had started to go through the video game story and the characters design. And to be true to oneself, it was refreshing to be hustling again. I found joy in hustling. Now I know it is true that if you find joy in what you do the stress would be joyful. But before I give myself fully back to work I had to work on spending more time with my family and how I would not let my wife remind me how little time I was spending with the family again. I had to live a life of balance. Balance is what we must all crave for. At some point in our life, we must balance everything. Some say balance signifies maturity, not that I agree or would disagree, but they have some point. A life of balance would excel in all spheres and be worth it, but a life not balanced will always give excuse of how it turned out to be, some are poor in this area because they wanted to be very good in that area. And excuses are bad for business. Right, you might not be able to strike a befitting balance for some activities in your life, but you should at least try. As I began the work back, I felt growth in the company – the time I took off did it and I needed it. Coming back to work, I also felt I needed to do more. I was reading a blog post at one time when I came across the words of the writer saying, "If you want to be successful you have to work more than anyone else". That was the basic truth, success comes to those who overwork, and not only overwork but overwork with smartness. I soon realized the difference between working hard and working smart. It has been a line that had not been clear to me but when it did I couldn't believe what I could achieve by being smart. When I took that break, I was willed to look inwards at myself and family. And the distance I have drifted from them was so evident I was broken. Thus, I thought of how I could merge my world together. I wanted to integrate my personal life with my hustle more so while spending time with my hustle I am also spending time with what matters – my family. This is a technique not everyone could apply. And not for all business. But if you could you should. I was going to put my business in my personal life and my personal life in my business.

I was very sure one may not be able to do this for every situation, but situations that we can do this for; my advice, do it – integrate your life with your livelihood and be smart about it. Being smart about everything would give you an edge over not being lost and hurt. It is true you could integrate your life with your family and hurt them both, there is no cookbook to guide against that, but you must be smart about it – somewhat providing a safety net. Surely if there is a way to make my personal life come to life in my hustle and there it was my wife. I have wanted to do something to get my wife involved, but never knew what it would be until then. Casheem, my wife, does hair; she does all types of braids and hairstyles. I talked to her and what she thought about being part of the company business-wise, "that's a good idea", she said. She wanted it. The thing I could not quite tell is who wanted it the most; She or I? Whatever the response we both wanted it. I mean that would be all that matters right? And she was good with the idea that I came up with, so we both have ourselves to each other, I knew it was going to be great for me; business-wise and family-wise. After discussing we both came up with her starting her own makeup brand. She went on to do research on it and I would take it from there. If I was going to do more, it would take more time and money to do it. And I was ready to. And I would not be doing for myself – not that I have been before – alone but with my family. I was going to have my family fight along with me. Such a wholesome experience it would be. Later years when the business would grow. I would appreciate this choice and look for more chances to get my family to work with me or that I may work with the family. Whichever way. With some time into the work; I publish the first issue of my magazine, Throne Magazine. I had previously employed blurb, I was still using their service and the journey to the publication couldn't be smoother. After I did [publication], my phone was buzzing every now and then. I had kept the magazine local and I did not really have something to move it as far as promoting it was concerned all I had were prints and digital copy; I promoted it myself. For promotion, I used social media for most of the part and the website I made for the company. After everything looked good and I was making ways. I had people wanting to do interviews and get involved now, but not many just a few. I was making impact, I got noticed by few investors also. Though no one talked about investing in me, just the friendly cues; letting me know they see what I was doing and from what it looks like to see if I fail or succeed. I was still disappointed with all those that wanted to talk but weren't going to put in. But was I heart-broken? No, at this point I was used to it. I had been built for this kind of world.

This would not be my first and not going to be my last – not that I anticipate it, but such was life. I was prepared for this I wouldn't blink. It did not feel different; my response was to grind more. I was going to be better and go on to my glorious future though wind blow against my ship I am going to ride on, though the light is out, I am going to use the stars. My all I would use, my blood I would spill until I surmount the great plains of tribulation and enter my dreams. I was not going to be distracted. Just mouthing; no help on the work nor with the money. I am still going to do great for myself. The launch of the magazine did great, but now I knew I should make more money through my company. I understood that business and I knew that I would not be a millionaire overnight it would take a lot of smart work and hard work. So, I began to look for ways that my business would make more. And the way for my business to make more was through sales. I need sales! I need to bring awareness to my brand, get more people wearing my brand, get big local names in the magazine. The video game was still in progress and so was the make-up line; it was going to take time to start making money over those. I must make more where I need to, to put money where I should, to get to the peak I want to. New product orders came in almost every month so now I need more space to hold my clothing line. My space was occupied with my equipment for music, so I talked to Kenneth Hoyt (DOT R) about it; I knew he was looking to go somewhere to set up his studio. When he had agreed, I gave all my equipment to him to use it as I would not be going into music anytime soon. Also, I wanted to get a new place for myself; with all the bills, taking care of the family and the business, I had to get a reasonable abode for myself. So, I spoke with him about getting a place together; and he was good with it. I really appreciate the role he played in my life at this point. I told him I would look for a place that would be appropriate for the both of us and then I would reach out to him. I can say with all clarity that knowing DOT R was one of the best things that happened to me; I have my uncle to thank for meeting him. He [DOT R] was there when I needed someone. He was a man of himself and understood me. There are times in life when we have people who are not from our bloodline become so close to us than we can ever imagine. My advice is that if you meet this sort of people, cling to them because they are rare. Friends that are closer than family. While I was going about doing my everyday work and minding my own business, I looked at my life and felt I was missing something. I often look at myself and realize that a void is left inside of me; you should to – look inwards.

And anytime I feel like this, I know the universe is telling me something; and the universe does speak in an encoded language to those who have the key, they decipher, and those who don't, just go circling. Such is life. I focused on myself and the universe to understand the times and what needs to be done. Then I realized that my answer had been staring in my face the whole time. That in life one would go through the good and the bad, but what one wants people to see more, the good or the bad? My answer was that I want people to see the good in me more often. I knew I had gone through some rough patches. Although my life might have been filled with so uncertainties my future may never be the one I wanted. I had scaled through. I had begun at a point of no hope, but I had ridden the horse that time gave and with elegance it has won the race. I had gone through the bad; I was going to speak forth the good it had brought forward. Thus, I began. I started to help others out and do positive things, though I have been left to work alone, I would want to be there for other people. And how did I come across the idea to help people out? It was from this guy, goes by the name Gary Vee – who actually felt like he was talking to me. I first heard him on the breakfast club where he was talking about sales and what to do to get income for your business, he grabbed my attention – he was my kind of speaker. So, I went on to search for his videos and I heard more talks on the subject of being positive and what it means. Being positive I realized is more than a sooth for the soul, it is a remedy for the soul. We are bound to be worried as long as the sun shines and bad things are certain to be happening day in day out but being positive in the midst of all these make you stand on top of the world. I know we would have heard of being positive daily, but hearing is never enough without doing. It took me long to realize how I had neglected the positivity factor in my business and everything else. I would later utilize my positivity in giving. I had been so focused on myself that I had neglected everyone around me. I had been so negative about people not helping me I was not lending a hand to help. But I realized I could change the direction and give even though I wasn't given. I would stretch out my hand in giving and it would be the bliss for me. I would give as a way to make a way for positivity in my life. It felt good helping people, I began to speak to people about the key factors in getting things done as far as their business goes. It is true I was helping. I could see the joy that comes from the smile I get, it was a comforting experience; for me and for them. I donated money, gave my time and tried ways to look out for anyone that needed me. I am still an evangelist for giving. I daily preach giving.

And in my years of sojourn I have seen and talked to people who believed until they get to a certain status or have a certain amount of time or money, they cannot give. If you are on such path; it's not the best. Yeah, there might be people that have done that, and it worked for them, but giving is one of the greatest ways to getting. I also believe that every one of us might not have money in excess to give or share, but we can all give our time – this we all have. Giving our time to others can go a long way to helping them and us in return. And let me tell you a basic truth; if one gives today, such person has planted a seed which would grow up someday to bear fruit for him or his children. I was giving to the best of my ability. But I would encounter a drawback with the business. I wasn't selling well. As time went by, sales were not increasing – I needed more sales, who doesn't? So, I focused my money on advertising and marketing to get the brand awareness up for Battle King Inc. Truly, without deceiving ourselves, sales are tough – have you ever tried it? Try it. With sales, one could never predict what will work with every customer; your best act is to do an overview of your entire customer base and do an approximation of the best sales act. But I was going to go through the fire, I was going to walk on the pegs, I was going to succeed. I would put in more money into getting the product to the world and a corresponding sale – law of proportionality – should come in. I should add that if only everything is done in the right way. I would look back at this time where I started from and how far I had gone and would tell myself, what a life I have lived. I would go on in later years to tell my story. I was nearing the end, and I would be having a fantastic story to tell – not everyone can get that opportunity.

"DON'T CARE ABOUT WHAT EVERYONE THINKS, IF YOU WANT TO DO IT THEN DO IT BECAUSE IF YOU DO IT OR DON'T THEY STILL WILL THINK THE SAME"

Eric Cominski Jr

Chapter 10

EVERY GOOD THING OR BAD HAS AN END. It is nearing the end of the day when men must go to sleep for the sun is about to sleep. I would recall the beginnings of the life I had lived. I would zoom into the distant past and stare at my present actions and I would realize how far I had gone with time. I was not getting younger. I was growing, and the fortitude of life was growing with me. I was happy with how far I had come. I am also sure that I am nearing my end with the certainty that I have been spent. Not that I would retire or something. I was just going to be living a life that is above strength. I had gotten the pegs in place, I had made it firm. I would just go on to do smart and greater things on it. As long as I recalled I have been a fighter. From the start, my life has been full of ups and downs. I had learned to roll with it or against it. I had learned to either go with the uncertainties that come with going against the storm or the certainty that comes with going with the storm. I had learned. I wouldn't say I have fared very well. Who even gives one that mark? But my life would tell of how much I have gone. My business would tell how long I have been better. I would only know how long I have fared with the success that is eminent from the business. I would remember when the creation blew the starting whistle and I was birthed into this world. The loneliness I felt and the distance I experienced with my father – the only one who could recognize the life of a man. That I detest at the time would go on to have prepared me for the future. As I sit back to look at my life. I realized that the most important lessons in them are the ones taught through life itself. Not the ones I learnt from school or audio and video tapes. It was the one I learned when we left our father, when I got my first job, when I started selling candy, when I was duped, when I was hated… They all have forged me into a man I had become today. Who will boldly start on the rooftop and say, "You see all this, and I made it happen". It is a man who is full of pride because of the dangers he had faced when he was humble. It is a man who at an early age has been stripped of innocence and the guilt that lay around him from everyone would go on to tell that he had a greater future. And I was that man. I had grown to become him. I navigated my life through the rivers of hardships; it was never easy for me – I agree– but it was worth it.

"If the things you face don't make you, they break you", those were the words that kept ringing in my head. Things I faced molded me, they broke me and made me up. I could remember times, tears as thick as the fog flooded my eyes. When I had no one to call my own. It was not always straight for me, and Yeah, I did get depressed… At one time, while I was starting my clothing line something happened. One of the T-shirt design I did have a negative feedback and it slowed down my sales afterward. If you've never been in this situation, you might be able to relate with how I felt this time. It was like waiting for your package to arrive and when it arrived, you got the long story version of how they were not able to deliver, and you could not do anything. That's was an abridged version of how I felt. Sales were making ways, but it took a downturn and my mouth began to water. And this was what happened. The T-Shirt that caused the whole down-drop for me was because of the design. It was called, "Throne" – a design of a guy sitting on a king-like chair with a gun in his hand. It was cool already, the production and design were great, but it came at around the time guns were being dubbed terrible. Guns were a terrible thing going around so many people did not buy the shirt. It was really hurting. Out of all the times, that guns can be branded terrible, my production time was that time. It was heavy on me as the sales of the shirt was bad. I really felt terrible at that time. I couldn't bear to lose in those times. And losing was knocking and I had started to turn off the door knobs as it was slowly walking in. I would remember this time as things got soiled for me. If I had so many sales options maybe it wouldn't have been that bad. But I didn't, all I had has been taken into the creating this elegant design which was at the time. I look back at that time, and I feel sorry for myself. After a while, when the whole thing died down, it picked up a little. And right, I could not have known how the situation of things would have been – I am not a soothsayer. I was just being creative, and I landed in that place. If I have a chance to do it again – make a design out of my creativity – I would. I would just learn if I fail. This struggle was very hard on me at this time, because I was just starting my clothing line. I assure you, it is not good for business. Believe me. At the start of the business, you would pray, hope and call for every help you can. As it gives you some sort of tenacious zeal, but if your first step in business goes into the ditch. What can the righteous do? It takes everything you have to stand and if you have people to go to, then you are at luck. I would also remember another fatal point in my career. It was my time with the magazine. I pointed out earlier the hurdles I had to face to get the magazine started: the pain in getting people to work with me on the magazine and all calls and no show.

It was not a smooth experience I would say, but it was interesting. After all my struggle with raising the magazine up to the standard of my brand. Although I got enough publicity with the publication of the magazine, it was not to its full potential. I would soon realize this after I had counted the cost and look back at what I did with clarity. It was not a total disaster as one would have thought, but it wasn't the standard you want for an entertainment magazine. With the magazine that was meant to help my sales, I couldn't get people to invest in me. So, you see why it faulted? Though I was reminded that people loved it. But no one loved it to a point that they want to put money into it. That was when I realize the fluke that it might have been. With all that was going on then, I would not classify it as a wreck that was unavoidable. It would have been better – I would think so – if I got better content. If I didn't make it go to personal and making it all about myself. Thus, it came to my thoughts in real time when people wouldn't want to join because I made it about me. The problem was not with me I soon found out, it was that I was just starting. No one knows me before. There is no pant to know me. So why make it about you? If I had made it about me when people wanted to know me, then it would have been perfect. But I still felt proud with all the dissatisfaction going around. In fact, I was able to steer it away from disaster on my own without any help from outsiders – which is a big plus for a one person building a magazine. To be true to everyone and myself, the magazine failed in content, though it could have done better if I had more help or if people could just show up. I didn't get much help in those days. But I fared. I was well and up without another hand to pull me up. I had to do the falling and standing myself. And anytime I fall, I have a series of things I do to bounce back. A technique that had helped over the years. I would give out some clothing to help others start their clothing lines, network with more people and work on getting a good team together. I had to do something, or I may never be able to face myself from defeat. All the things I did was my way of stepping back and looking at the entire picture. At some point in our life, when failure has dawned on us. We may want to escape. We may be tempted to pad failure and look for an excuse to hold on to. But that we may, doesn't mean we should. And if we unluckily do "may", we end up losing more than the substance. We lose ourselves, our dreams, passion, glory… There are less of books out there that teaches one how to deal with failure of any kind. And the few ones that do have more difference than similarity with the problem you are facing. Man can never be able to decipher the perfect recipe for dealing with failure.

But if we could look inward, focus on positivity, avoid negative energy, and surround yourself with life…we might live to tell the tales of our life. Most people think that the solution is out there. In the books, on the internet, the videos, and audios. But it might be shocking they might not be ours. It is true they give us a hint, it is always an opinion from one side of the table, the table that can never see all. I believe all the information out there is extremely valuable and can never be weighed. But when we get to these points of realization, in the heat of the moment, when life experiences are more real than they describe in the book. Then we know how far from the reality we have made our mind wonder. When betrayal saps our strength and no human effort could seem to bring us back, then we realize how far away from the answer we stood. The truth, no one has a definite answer to our problems not even ourselves. We can only learn and hope to be better by the day. One of the biggest failures for me is putting a team together. All through my business endeavor, I felt no one believed in me – no one was in on my dreams. I had let them be because they didn't believe in the same dreams that I had. I had not gone on to find if there was a third option of my dreams and their's coming together. I didn't think that they not filling in with my dream was a sign of strength and not of weakness. Also, another thing was the fact that I wasn't very social – I stayed to myself because of how I grew up. I could never trust many. This is one of the attributes I would advise anyone that has to knock out bit by bit. If you would be an entrepreneur, you would never be around to monitor everything – a plain truth – and without trust – at least a single person – you might end up miserable. And this can be a menace, not only to you but to everyone around you. Then from there, you begin leading people to the ditch. I tried my best to be a better version of myself and strip myself of the attitudes that I know can deter. And when I started getting better with people I realized that most people are full of shit. When I discovered that I need to interact more and network more. I began and the people I talked to – maybe I was talking to the wrong people, but how could I be talking to the wrong people every time, what are the odds? – I got nothing from them. And those who were able to relate with me were not ready to be part of me. It is always expedient to note that these are my honest advice; though I have not been in all situations, I have been in most situations you can think of as an entrepreneur. My ink is leveling down. My back aches in this acacia chair that I sit in. The sun is going to sleep, it is TIME TO SAY GOODBYE. I have lived for little years, but I have seen endless things.

I have said goodbyes I would love to take back, I have said join me I would love was true, but all the way I am where I am. When I started on the part to be great, I had one thing in mind – making money. I know most people are of the opinion that your aim should not be to make money – I for one would not argue about it. But I am telling you from my own natively colored outlook of how I viewed life. I realized at a very tender age what money could do and not do. I saw at first hand from laying hands on my first business till today how money is so important. To state they fact, we can never decide without it on ground. Money says do not make decisions when I am not at home. A proverb among the locals in my county. What I saw in my first experience with life was how money could be so critical that life might not be worth living without it. I would go on in life to learn lessons that it was not about money. It was more than. But we could never ever drop the influence of money in business. At that time all I thought about was making money because that was what the environment around me was saying. So, all I could ever think about was making more money – I am not justifying myself, just stating the facts. Throughout my entire neighborhood then, people would not know you if you volunteered to help clean the community or you help clear the garden, not that they would not thank you. They would and the next time you meet, they would be like, "what is that your name again". But this I have seen. A man set up a party in the neighborhood and people would go on to tell of its tales every day. That was what the environment has thought me. I would go on to unlearn what my environment taught me about money and learn that everything is not and should not be about money. Not that I can say emphatically that everything should not be about money, but making money alongside doing good or offering some services or product to the society is not beyond what one should aim for. One thing that I learnt in my years of interacting with Mother Nature is that being poor might be expensive. Yeah, you heard that right, "It is expensive to be poor". When I tell people this; they would be like What? What do you mean? I got this while I was reading an article on one of the microblogging platforms. The article itself was titled: WHY IT IS SO EXPENSIVE TO BE POOR. At first, the title felt strange, which is what I would believe captivated me, and I wanted to know more. I wanted to know what he meant or didn't mean. It was also a shock to me then but after I read it, it made more sense than I might have wondered. In the best of my knowledge, I would like to paint a scenario of this sort of situation for you. Let us assume that you broke your car's taillight, you could not fix it because it would cost more than you can afford at the moment. A few days later, you are on your way to work, and you were flag by the policemen about your taillight and from there things can get really messy so that at the end, the cost of fixing the tail light at the first instance is nothing compared to the total cost of running errand for the police. That one could be a less extreme situation. But you can go on further to create some of this scenario yourself and you would learn the lesson of this. Thus, I conclude, not having money can be a problem, being so focused on making money can be described as illness. Some I have seen would still go on to the being stiff with the money. They are so focused on making money, they wouldn't want to give out. And at the end of the day, they would realize that at the end of the day, the so much precious money could not give them all they wanted. There is always a high calling for everyone that wants to make money. And the calling is definitely not money. When I discovered this truth about money. It would go on to change my life forever. It was a moment of self-discovering. Self-discovering was more of a blessing to me and has helped me navigate through the storms that had risen all through my journey. It made me stay focus. I did lose focus sometimes, but then I realize the mountain I have been climbing is nothing but sand. Self-discovery or self- realization – finding oneself – is what made me realize what I had been searching for so long as always being within my reach. It was it [self-discovery] that help me recognize the green pastures that are near instead of the ones I had focused on that are far. It was this that taught me that with little learning and work, I can go on to create a new world of mine own. In the process of self-discovery, I had to remind myself of the future I want, and I still do until this day. You've got to find a way or ways to remind yourself. It could be people, things, experience, pain…anything you could employ its service to remind you of the future you want. If you wouldn't have people or things that would remind you of the future you want, you would become comfortable with the place you are in. The mediocre would seem like the end you wanted. You would toil in the sun believing that the future you always wanted is here. All the while the future is far off. And if by chance a miracle happens before life has ended and you realize how far you have deviated from the initial dreams that gave you goosebumps. Then you could go out to reach for it, else you would have to leave with the choices you have made. In the end, we all have to leave with the choices we made. We could all have wished for the better and wished we had made better choices, but we can't change anything. It is sealed in the history of times. Men might laugh at our decisions, they may curse it, or they may bless it. Whichever they do, we would still have made that decision – nothing will change it. The power now comes in our abilities to leave with the story we have written. I am living with mine. I would not deny it, which is what I see most people trying to do, deny the existence of that bad choice that got you fired. No, you shouldn't, you should own it. When you own it, then it wouldn't hurt. The pain you feel hurts becomes it has not been part of you. But when you own it, it wouldn't hurt. So, no matter what you plan to do; strive for success but when you have made terrible choices own it. Do not blame the time or the traffic, own it straight up, it is your only savior. And at the end, you are going to shine. Ever true as I pen the journey down. I have experienced all this emotion again. I have laughed hard, cried more, smile much more. It was a tale I want to tell the world. When I began the journey, I had no one – apart from my mom and wife. Then along the way, I met this great guy whom I got connected to at my old job. He was a work of art and understands me very well – at least I would think so. His ways were more like mine and he helped me a lot. He would help me get great deals on the clothing brand. He was one of the few that believe in me. I still salute his ways in my life till this day. Kenneth Hoyt, DOT R, my man, also came along the ride. He came at a timely moment and his entry has been a great one with effect. He was older than I was, but he understood the zeal I had, and believe in my dreams and wanted to be part of it. Who then said, "Three is a crowd"? Maybe I could have had more people to talk about if I was indifferent to the society. But then I have to plea my stand, that the society at a very young age taught me to trust a selected few. The society taught me to run by the rules and avoid outside of line discussion. Right from time, I knew I did not belong to the crowd – I could not help it. Mixing with the crowd was never a strong suit of mine which I would say help me along my way because every time I received a cold response from people, I reminded myself that it was part of the human instinct and was not new. I would not say this attitude of mine is the best, or the worst. I have come to know myself – my strengths and weaknesses – and I have come to dwell with the strength and that was always ready when people said no. Not many people are like that – we are designed specifically different – but we must all learn. And as the saying goes, "life is not a bed of roses" the earlier you realize this and find yourself the best advantage point to combat life through the worst and through the better. I had combat life happily with the tools that are not from birth, but the ones that I got in this life. My plan was and still is to build a formidable team for my company – I know it would take longer, but I am ready to take all the chances. I would like to get the magazine established more.

The magazine I am convinced would be a big thing. I want to get my wife more involved in the business, it was going to be nice to have her all around. My wife is an amazing woman in my life already, and if I am lucky to have her in my business as in my life, I would be the luckiest man on the planet. I still have years to live for, I would go on to accomplish the head of the best and be well known in Virginia as far as in all the business that I am known for. Recently, I just began my own Cigar Brand, Crown Cigars. I have been giving out samples for feedback before I do a big order – testing the waters before plunging, an awesome technique you should always employ. Also, it happened that at this time I want to get into the music arena – I was going to come back any time and this time seemed the best. I am currently working on my album. I have waited for it all to come true, and day by day it is. What a wait! I have started off small, but I was on to bigger things. I had my Battle King Inc. which is the company that has all my hustles under it. Battle King Clothing a clothing line, Throne Magazine, Royalty Unleashed Gaming the video game studio, Casheem Makeup line Queen Beauty and on to better things than I would ever have dreamed of. I am never going to give up and settle for a life with ease. I am going to reach far beyond the stars to the horizon human mind could not accommodate. I am going to just go for it. THE SONG over the radio that played all through my journey as began and its fulfillment is a joy to hear so I sang along.

"...We shall overcome,

We shall overcome someday,

Oh, deep in my heart, I do believe,

We shall overcome someday..."

[the song trailed off]

END

"THANK YOU TO EVERYONE WHO HELP ME IN THE SMALLEST WAY BECAUSE EVERY MOMENT COUNTED FOR WHERE I'M AT NOW"

Eric Cominski Jr

www.ingramcontent.com/pod-product-compliance
Lightning Source LLC
Chambersburg PA
CBHW050634150426
42811CB00052B/796